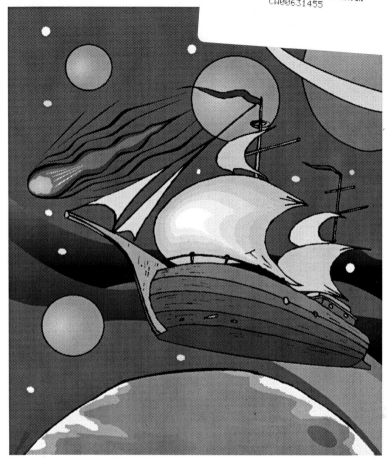

2001: A POETRY ODYSSEY DERBYSHIRE

Edited by Dave Thomas

First published in Great Britain in 2001 by
YOUNG WRITERS
Remus House,
Coltsfoot Drive,
Peterborough, PE2 9JX
Telephone (01733) 890066

HB ISBN 0 75432 936 4
SB ISBN 0 75432 937 2

FOREWORD

Young Writers was established in 1991 with the aim to promote creative writing in children, to make reading and writing poetry fun.

This year the 2001: A Poetry Odyssey competition again proved to be a tremendous success with over 50,000 entries received nationwide.

The amount of hard work and effort put into each entry impressed us all, and is reflective of the teaching skills in schools today.

The task of selecting poems for publication was a difficult one but nevertheless, an enjoyable experience. We hope you are as pleased with the final selection in *2001: A Poetry Odyssey Derbyshire* as we are.

CONTENTS

Lisa Wilson	82
Toni Glover	82
James Wootton	83
Alexandria Smith	83
Charlotte Hinde	84
Laura Baldwin	85
Rebecca Taylor	86
Emma Ashmore	86
Amie Smith	87
Alison Christian	88
Allen Pickering	88
Arran Lange	89
Kingsley Davies	89
Ben Stacey	89
Emma Bradshaw	90
Scott Thomas	90
Donna Hoskin	91
Matt Angus	92
Sarah Farris	93
Jacqueline Smith	94
Katie Simpson	94
Mark Gascoyne	95
Emma Lankford	95
Sally Davies	96
Ben Watkinson	97
Chantelle Oldfield	97
Kelli Cocking	98
Paul Murphy	98
Philippa Brown	99
Robert Ward	100
Stephen Barnett	100
Tom Fisher	101
Rachel Barratt	102
Rebecca Yeowart	102
Laura Blissett	103
Elizabeth Huggins	103
Kourtney Yates	104
Laura Grimwade	104

Ryan Kemp	105
Matthew Taylor	105
Angharad Stanley	106
Anya Taylor	106
Emma Mellor	107
Lauren Tailby	108
Sam Walker	108
Hannah Scott	109
Luke Preston	109
Kelly Cotterill	110
Daniel Barker	110
Jack Needham	111
Dannie Methven	112
Robert Garner	112
Emma Swale	113
Jodie Fareham	113
Gemma Sellars	114
Rebecca Platts	114
Franco Hardy	115
James Watkinson	116
Aden Carlile	116
Michelle Prince	117
Lindsey Starkey	118
Emma Greenwood	118
Stephanie Krence	119
Laura Jennison	120
Rebecca Page	120
Amy Read	121
Phoebe Woods	122
Karen Dove	122
Debbie Davies	123
Lucy Chambers	124
Kathryn Shedden	125
Jonathan Dean Carver	126
Dean Mitchell	126
Richard Pyatt	127
Kristopher Kemp	128
Kylie Bonsell	128

The Poems

I AM WHO I AM

I am who I am
But no one else
I am in the future, which will be the past
I am who I am

I am who I am
But no one else, just myself
I am who I am, just like a tiny ant
I am who I am

I am who I am
Lying down on my bed in a world of my own
Looking at the stars, wishing there was someone in my world
I am who I am

I am who I am
But no one else
I am in my world in my galaxy, thinking what a lovely world of mine
I am who I am

I am who I am
Sleeping on my bed
Dreaming about myself about what a lovely person I am
I am who I am.

Edward Gentry (13)
Alderwasley Hall School

ALWAYS MOVING, NEVER STOPPING

They say life is like a roller-coaster,
It's not.
For most of us, it's more like a Ferris wheel.
It keeps on moving, round and round.
Always moving, never stopping.
Just the same old thing,
Always moving, never stopping.

Don't get me wrong, it's not a bad thing.
I like Ferris wheels, so do loads of people.
Very relaxing, in fact.
But after a while it gets tedious.
Always moving, never stopping.

A man I know, works in an office.
He gets up, gets dressed, goes to work, comes home, goes to bed.
Every day, apart from Sunday.
On Sunday, he sleeps.
Every week of his life is like this.
Going round, like a Ferris wheel.
Always moving, never stopping.

Craig Chisholm (13)
Alderwasley Hall School

THE JOURNEY OF THE COBRA

A snake in the hot sand.
He waits for the bird that stalks the sky.
Who brings death to all around it.
And he waits for the wild beast to flee.

Now he gets up from the sand and goes on
His journey to his real home in the rainforest near the
Congo where his family live.
But he still has a long way to go and a lot of danger
Ahead of him.
The snake is actually a cobra and he reaches
The border between the desert and the rainforest.
He finds his family two metres away and just
When he gets there a tiger jumps out of the hedges.
The cobra attacks the tiger
But, it was not enough to kill it.
His family attacks the tiger with all their might
To kill the tiger and they did kill it.
The family was reunited and ate the tiger, then look up
And gaze at the stars above.

Matt Walton (13)
Alderwasley Hall School

WHAT TO DO NEXT!

Why do we sit there wondering what's happening next.
So there we are chatting on the phone
Wondering what to do next.
I sit there watching TV and seeing what's on.

Wondering what to do next!

I lay there asleep having a dream
A dream about a holiday
Wondering where to go.
So I go outside thinking

Wondering what to do next!

I sit there thinking looking out the window
Watching the rain steadily pouring down.

Wondering what to do next!

I go and put my raincoat and feel what it's like.

Wondering what to do next!

Craig Johnstone (13)
Alderwasley Hall School

BORING SCHOOL

I was just sitting there staring into dull space.
Daydreaming and peering at the children around me.
I couldn't get gloomy colours out of my mind,
Dark blue, dark purple, grey, black and brown.
It had seemed like
Days, weeks even years since this morning started.
But I keep thinking to myself when this dull school finishes . . .

Jennie-Marie Stone (11)
Ecclesbourne School

THE SPARKLING SEA

The bashing tide came in,
Crashing and spilling over the rocks,
Takes control of the ships like feathers,
Comes down like vultures to catch its prey,
Sparkling with dozens of silver fish,
Pushing all different creatures inshore,
Seaweed grabbing your feet like hands,
Wetting everything around,
splash,
Seagulls screaming above your head,
Suddenly nothing.

Cameron Hughes (11)
Ecclesbourne School

THE SEA STORM

Blue waves crashing upon the shore
Windsurfers riding the waves,
The sky turning grey like a storm starting,
Lifeguards man their sea crafts,
Red flags flying high like a bird,
Dogs terrified of the storm force,
Little baby upon the shore,
Parents worried their baby's drowning,
Cats horrified at the raging water,
I love the storm.

Jack Ellis (11)
Ecclesbourne School

Village Fete

A village fete, as merry as an exploding party,
A wild beacon of fun and laughter.
Fancy dress with yellows, reds and blues,
Everything so mad and exciting.
So great, so vast and exotic,
It's so extremely noisy but nobody cares because they're all
having lots of fun.
Coconuts are smashed and prizes are won.
A wonderful time to be had by everyone,
Enjoyment ran around and excited the crowd.
Then, suddenly, like a power cut . . .

Tom Gough (11)
Ecclesbourne School

Waves

The waves crash
As they come in,
Hissing, swishing and swashing.
The tide comes in
Tumbling, tossing and crashing
Against the cliff,
Sounding like thunder,
Reaching fifty feet towards the sky.
'It's getting out of control'
Demolishing anything
That gets in its path.
It suddenly stops,
You can hear the seagulls
Calling from afar.

Aaron Noble (11)
Ecclesbourne School

AUTUMN

Darkness fills the skies on those short autumn days,
The sun is hidden behind a thick layer of cloud.
Golden leaves fall off the trees,
Winter is just around the corner.

Fires are turned on, the nights start to get cold,
Fireworks light up the dark night,
Mist fills the street,
A thick blanket of velvet lies over the world,
A fresh sparkle of dew lies on spiders' webs,
All the animals are hibernating and the streets are empty,
. . . It's autumn.

Holly Cooke (12)
Ecclesbourne School

TOWN THROUGH WINDOW

So busy -
Busy as the January sales.
Everyone is occupied.
Air bunged up
Smothering.
Dreary
Drab
Narrow spaces.
Scurrying figures -
Like a black and white film.
Overcast as ceiling tiles.
Shoppers catching the shops -
Before they shut.
Nothing is still.

Sophie Andersen (12)
Ecclesbourne School

MIDNIGHT MOON

Her long fingers brush the sea
Making it curl like a snail's shell.
Her long tresses flow behind her
Blowing the calm quiet sea.
Soon she walks away
Leaving only a gentle breeze
To make the grey clouds slowly drift
Over the sky.
The moon tucks itself
Under the warm woolly clouds
Making the sea turn a midnight blue.
The crying seagulls soon disappear
Leaving only the soft, sweet sound
of the lapping waves!

Daniella Trifunovic (11)
Ecclesbourne School

THE CAT

He is the king
The cat
In his cape of black
The cat
He takes no captives.
The cat
Slaughters his prey
The cat
Likes to torment his victims
The cat
As mighty as the lion.

Jonathan Hatchett (12)
Ecclesbourne School

THE FEAR

I am the fear struck into your heart,
bravery has been torn apart!

I am the sound of a bottled up shriek,
It's so loud you can feel it in your feet!

I am the darkness choking the light,
If you can think I can't scare you, well I just might!

I am the thin line between pleasure and pain,
enough of the pleasure, terror must reign!

I am the horror caged away,
now that I'm back I'm here to stay!

I am the nightmare waiting to bite,
go to sleep and I'll give you a fright!

And so you can see I am the fear,
When your hairs stand up you know I am near!

Daniel Mitchell (12)
Ecclesbourne School

ANGER IS . . .

An explosion trying to get out.
A grey cloud plundering the blue sky.
The lightning in the heavens.
The crumbling noise of thunder.
A lit bomb ready to explode.
A child screaming loud enough to deafen.
An earthquake breaking the world.
A fierce tiger which has escaped.
Desperately wanting a companion to stop!

Victoria Hickling (12)
Ecclesbourne School

AUTUMN DAYS

A utumn is here,
U nderground, animals begin to hibernate,
T ree leaves are falling and scatter many different colours.
U nder the slate-coloured clouds the rain falls,
M um buys fresh, crunchy apples,
N ever-ending conker matches.

D ark blue blackberries just outside the window,
A ll migrating birds fly south,
Y ucca trees start to wither,
S hort days are just around the corner, the long days retreat.

R ipe berries hang in bunches,
E arly morning mists, gloom,
T ractors are busy collecting the harvest,
U mpires close up the wickets until next season,
R eturn of crisp morning air,
N ature continues her seasonal changes.

Will Borrington (12)
Ecclesbourne School

RACE

Excitement captured in their hearts, displayed on their scarlet faces.
The shouts of the crowd cheer them on as they aim for the finish.
Their feet pounding the ground like a hammer.
Their hair brushed back from their faces by the howling wind
As they speed across the ground like a bullet.
The intense noise pounding in their ears violently -
And the quick slap of their feet on the freezing tarmac, hidden,
Taken over by the shouts.

Rebecca Douglas (11)
Ecclesbourne School

PEACE

Bright sunshine filters through
Soft sponge clouds
In the clear blue sky
The water glistens like diamonds
As they dance upon the sea's
Surface
A wispy cloud moves
Across the settled sky
A light shadow like the silhouette of a
Misty man
Moves through the still water
Shadows are cast on the seashore
As the water ripples over the golden sand
Shells rock on the sea bed
A light breeze that dares
To stir a calm warm day!
Glides silently through the thin air . . .

Kate Luing (11)
Ecclesbourne School

DARK SEA SPRAY

The sky was black like an eclipse of the once bright sun,
The fierce wind was striking the tall cliff like cars crashing
                                        into one another,
The long beaches were heavily deserted, the sand washing out to sea,
The strong water was crashing hard against the slippery rocks
and the sea spray was flying off onto the deserted beach like heavy rain,
The tall boats waved slowly on the sea and the seagulls were
                                        nowhere to be seen.
This night was darkest black, the sea rough and the sea spray
                                        was everywhere.

Alex Minion (11)
Ecclesbourne School

WHAT A MATCH!

It's the opposition's penalty,
The keeper pulls off an amazing dive to keep the score 0-0,
But now it's their corner,
What a header and it's in the back of the net,
The score is now 1-0 to them,
There is continuous pressure on the opposition,
But the ball just will not go in the back of the net,
There are twenty seconds left and it's a corner,
The goalkeeper quickly moves up field hoping to snatch a goal,
The corner swings in,
It's the keeper who made contact . . . *goal!*
It is 1-1 and there are five seconds remaining,
The opposition take kick-off but they get tackled,
The centre forward shoots from way out,
It soars through the air as fast as a bullet towards the goal . . . *it's in!*
The crowd roared like a frustrated tiger,
And then the ref blew his whistle so hard he went red,
The fat lady is singing now - it's all over,
What a match!
We'll be back with Terry Venables and Gary Lineker after a short
break.

Josh Turner (11)
Ecclesbourne School

AUTUMN

Autumn is the rage of the dark clouds,
Autumn is the look on people's faces when summer's over
Autumn is all the grief and anger of the world we live in
Autumn is the hair salon that cuts and dyes the trees.

Michael Little (13)
Ecclesbourne School

The Winter's Evening

Snowflakes and ice fall in a silver storm,
While white snow encases the spindly tree
and the glistening rooftops with an icy, cold sheet.
Through the pallid steamed up windows,
Orangey yellow fires flow merrily from the grate,
And dance about, licking up at the sooty black chimney.
Dust grey smoke invades the streamers of white
Falling from the cold sky scattering them wildly,
But under a lonely willow, next to the frozen stream,
A tiny rose stands bravely, fighting
Through the deathly cold, snow and ice,
Just a tiny speck of red in the whiteness of the world.

Claudia Lennox (12)
Ecclesbourne School

Bat

I am the king of darkness
Prince of the night sky
All prey is at my mercy
Nothing can escape
Nothing can hide

Nothing can even run.
I have wings of solid steel
And a body like rock.
Moths die when they hear my name.
I am king predator
I am king assassin
I am king bat.

James Campbell (12)
Ecclesbourne School

AUTUMN

I like
The flame and golden leaves
The crisp
Refreshing mornings
The cool sunny days
The steel spider webs,
Wet with dew.
I like
The thick ashen frost
The bare jagged trees
The conkers falling like stones
From the trees
Their fall broken by
The spiky green quilts.
I like
The shiny glint from
The frosty floor
The light brown
And the stuck car door
I like
Autumn.

Steven Moore (12)
Ecclesbourne School

FRIGHTENED I AMS

I am the spiders crawling on the dark, webbed walls.
I am the footsteps of the grey stranger.
I am the wings of the long, black bat.
I am the leaf of the tree in the lonely town.
I am the sparkle on the sharp knife.
I am the tapping of the door in the attic.

Bryony Farrar (12)
Ecclesbourne School

TIGER

Tiger, king of the jungle
Tiger, king of the predators
Tiger the beautiful and
admirable killer.
He can kill a human
in one quick bite,
He has no need of guns
to kill
His teeth are iron daggers
He can stalk and shadow his prey
day or night.
So is he really
pussycat
or an elegant and
captivating killer,
Tiger, king of the jungle
Tiger, king of the predators.

James Rickerby (12)
Ecclesbourne School

CALM

The dark blue sea as dead as a skeleton.
Not moving,
The blazing sun,
Yellowy-gold, burning the sand.
No clouds,
Blue sky,
The beach as empty as the Sahara desert.
Creatures,
Undisturbed,
The surfers turn their backs.

George Kelly (11)
Ecclesbourne School

ELEPHANT

I am sultan of the African plains,
I am Rajah of the whole of India,
King of all the beasts.

I get first pick of all the luscious leaves
and a mud pool to myself.

I am the mighty giant Goliath,
Challenging my enemies,
Trampling down the grass as if
I was a tornado tearing down a city.

I am a knight; my skin is my armour,
I am a warrior; my trunk is my club,
my tusks, spears.
I'm protecting my land against thieving lions.

I am wild, no one can tame me.
No man or circus can.

Eleanor Gardner (12)
Ecclesbourne School

STORMY DAY

The sea is stormy,
The sky is as black as a deep, black hole,
Ships being tossed around like feathers,
The sailors scattered around,
The water as cold as ice,
The winds blowing like slashing knives,
Boats colliding with the rocks,
Too strong to be tamed,
Endlessly thrashing nature and man,
Beautiful but cruel.

Mike Waterson (11)
Ecclesbourne School

TITANIC

It was a tranquil hazy night
Everyone was relaxing
When this tragic happening occurred
Then suddenly from the crow's nest *iceberg ahead, turn!*
But it was too late.
They thought they would make it, but they did not know
A few hours later they realised that the beautiful ship would
Be no more.
Women and children first!
The fights to the boats were like pirates to treasure
Men being shot for trying to get on the boats,
Children screaming for their fathers to come,
Women sobbing for their husbands.
Then when the ship started sinking it broke in two!
The bow went down, but the stern bobbed like a cork for an hour or two
And finally went down into the cold depths,
Cold like an ice demon, having its bath in sub zero water.
Then all was tranquil and hazy again.

Emily James (11)
Ecclesbourne School

THE HORIZON

The horizon was shining like a lantern
over the big, industrial estate.
The noise of cars echoed around my house.
The flats are as grey as an elephant.
When I went in the estate was quiet,
the sun went down, the street was dead, so was my house.
Until the next sunrise.

Marcus Sinkinson (11)
Ecclesbourne School

HAPPY

I am the smile on a circus clown's face,
The dawn of a bright new day,
The laughter of a stand up comedian's audience,
I am the tweet of a bird's song on a high tree,
The touch of a brand new pillow,
The first step on a beautiful Miami beach,
I am the sight of fireworks that explode
In the deep blue sky,
The sound of a good piece of advice,
The best friend you never had
I am the newborn flower in the fresh watered soil,
The song that you love,
The touch of fur on a carpet,
I am your favourite dream.

Isabel Hanslow (12)
Ecclesbourne School

THE COUNTRYSIDE

The fields a deep green
with animals scattered around.
The sun as red as ruby
as it rises behind the clouds.
The tree swaying in the breeze
with all the different shades of green.
The stream gently flows along with the kingfishers
skimming the glistening surface.
In the distance the meadow is like a
golden carpet full of buttercups,
The farmer sowing the seeds for another year.

Vicky Henman (11)
Ecclesbourne School

FEAR

I take a deep breath before I enter,
Tremble as I suspect what's inside.
The silence is deafening,
The darkness is fatal.
Before I enter the chamber of fear.

My arm shakes as I reach for the jail door,
Why am I entering this prison cell?
The door swings open.
I step fearfully inside,
The door clicks shut . . . I'm trapped to my destiny.

I stand stock-still in the middle of the room,
The darkness wrapping around me.
What should I do?
Should I reach out?
The light switch is a saviour.

My arm reaches out and on goes the light,
I breathe a temporary sigh of relief.
But now I know,
I have to look across.
To confront my scariest fear.

There it is, prowling along.
My trembling is an earthquake.
A hairy monster,
A modern T-rex,
The spider in the bath!

Tom Howell (13)
Ecclesbourne School

MODERN TIMES

Traffic jam,
An industrial metropolis,
Grey,
Increasing punctures in the ozone layer,
On a blisteringly hot day,
Scorching like a white hot oven,
Children getting agitated,
Everyone becoming restless,
Tension building like a thermometer rising,
Yellow, as the sun burns downward.
Queues for miles,
All because of a duo of old pensioners.

David Oakley (11)
Ecclesbourne School

THE SEA

The blue sea gets angry,
He begins to fight like a lion
catching its prey,
Fishermen begin to feel sick,
Babies begin to cry,
He swallows up the beach,
The deadly killer moves on,
He starts attacking a hard innocent soul,
Everybody races back home,
He starts to calm down,
As calm as a statue,
You would never know he was a killer.

Emma Street (11)
Ecclesbourne School

Autumn

Autumn means conker season,
Chestnut brown and ivory centred,
These little gems are what make autumn for me,
Along with amber and cherry leaves that litter the floor,
Dahlias, ruby bright and elegant, great in the morning sun,
Frost makes paths and roads sparkle like diamonds,
Birds' choruses drift away as dawn turns to day,
Animals hibernate underground,
Warm and snug in their little homes,
Lakes turn to glass, littered with cracks where children try to
crack the ice,
Nights get longer, days get shorter, the sky is ebony black
by eight o'clock,
Misty mornings make drivers cautious and careful.
Rivers stop flowing,
Plants wither and die,
Signs that autumn is here.

Ross McCabe (12)
Ecclesbourne School

The Sea

Sometimes the sea is motionless,
Like a mouse asleep,
In its little, hidey-hole.
The silver sea is just the fishes,
Having the time of their lives.
Sometimes the sea is as tough
And big and scary as a T-Rex.
As it gets stormy,
It can be destructive and wild,
Like an African lion.

Edward Witten (11)
Ecclesbourne School

AUTUMN

Look what happens when autumn strikes!
Autumn is when,
Football starts
The blossomed flowers disappear
Animals hibernate
Warm fires are lit
Blackberries hang on their bushes
Waiting to be eaten,
The last bee echoes through the
Empty meadow,
The fire is turned up,
Some sort of animal is rustling in
The dead leaves,
There is the smell of wet rotting
Leaves,
People sit in their houses
Watching the rain,
Day turns to night with just a blink
Of an eye and
Hot chocolate gets hotter.

Jonathan Kennedy (12)
Ecclesbourne School

BIG APPLE

The tall buildings stand high in the sky,
As tall as I have ever seen.
The pollution from the cars below rises up and
Gets trapped in-between.

The streets are full of people
Leading very busy lives.
Many of them live in fear of possible
Muggers and their knives.

They say that many famous people live
Here in this big city.
I believe a man called John Lennon
Was shot here; that was a pity.

There's a tall statue that stands in Manhattan
Alone and so high
In one hand she holds a set of scales
And in the other a torch that points towards the sky.

Richard Lidsey (11)
Ecclesbourne School

TORNADO

At the darkest point of the night
Something big is coming.
The sky is as dark as a shallow cave.
A tornado!
It destroys everything in its path
Maybe it's as gigantic as a brick boulder
And as tall as a bleak, grey skyscraper,
Towering over a tiny ant.
It kicks helpless little tiles off terrified roofs
Like Frisbees.
Flying into shattering windows.
Screaming can be heard from miles away
But nothing can be done.
As the violent, swirling, wild wind
Heaves itself around a poor, helpless city.
The dark, stormy sky becomes darker
And even more miserable.
As the tornado whirls past the city
it moves on for more revenge!

Amy Dormer (11)
Ecclesbourne School

AUTUMN

I looked out of my window early one morning,
I saw the cold mist surrounding me,
I heard birds singing as I looked out of my window
and the cold air sneaking through my floorboards,
The fresh twinkle of frost on a spider's web,
The trees were nearly bare,
Eventually the days turn colder and shorter, having
to stay indoors to wrap up warm next to a red hot fire,
The colours in flowers were fading,
leaves were falling to the ground,
I saw the fresh dew across the meadow shining in the sunlight,
The sky turns into a dark slate mist.

Leanne Hill (12)
Ecclesbourne School

THE SEA

All the beaches were wet
the sky was turning black.
Rain thrashed down on the sea
the tide was high and hostile.
All the grey clouds were taking over the sky.
The sea looked like a furious bear on a rampage.
Rocks were covered in thick, salty water.
Sea water was dark blue seizing at the rocks
and then pushing them down to the bottom of the sea.
The fish were scattering from their groups
swimming in and out of the waves.
Then all is quiet.

John Purves (11)
Ecclesbourne School

AUTUMN

I am autumn,
The bright colours
Of crunchy leaves.
The sun that hails
An early dawn.
I am autumn,
The spiny conkers
And harvest.
The warm fires
And hot-water bottles.
I am autumn,
The short days
And bonfire night.
The silhouetted horizon
At dusk.
I am autumn,
Migration
And hibernation,
The blackberry pickers
With stained fingers.
I am autumn,
The frosty grass
In the morning,
And seeing your own breath
As it hangs and fades.

Rachel Scothern (12)
Ecclesbourne School

RIDING IN THE COUNTRY

Riding in the country the sound so charming.
Yellow crops swaying in the breeze.
Thundering hooves as loud as thunder.
Galloping through the wind, hair gliding back freely.
The wind flying by silent as a mouse.
Just a murmur.
The sun the graceful lord of the sky.
Hangs above us.
So dazzling that it blinds you.
A blob appears puzzling to some,
It's just a black shape some say.
The blob thing follows you, it's alive, moving.
It's scary, it's alive, then disappears without a trace,
As you enter the undergrowth of the tree.
There's running water as graceful as a swan.
As you reach the woods a canter picks up.
Rough, brown logs to jump, clear blue streams.
The wood flies by gradually getting faster.
Faster and faster, it's getting darker.
Getting slower and slower, sweat running.
Time to go home.

Chloe Bennett (11)
Ecclesbourne School

AUTUMN

Animals hibernating
Under a starry sky
Trees with no leaves
Under a cool cloudy sky
Many leaves falling to the ground
Never a dull colour in autumn

Short sunny days
Evenings with full moons
A silvery spider's web covered in dew
Slowly rising sun glinting on the fresh frost
Ochre, cinnabar and golden leaves
Never a dull colour in autumn.

Caroline Shepherd (12)
Ecclesbourne School

AUTUMN

Autumn is when the trees go bare,
When the plants begin to die,
Leaves on the floor crisp and rust,
Fires light homes glowing scarlet and gold.

Autumn is when the birds fly south,
When the spider's web is silver.
There's a snap of a twig,
As animals go to hide. For winter is near.

Autumn is when the days are short,
It's cold and there's mist,
The floor glimmers with frost;
Everyone wraps up warm.

Autumn is when acorns fall,
When the conkers crack
And the blackberries are ripe.
We can see ourselves breathe when we scurry outside.

Autumn is when there's fruit from the harvest.
Halloween is nearby
And bonfire night's not too far ahead.
Autumn is crimson, ochre, yellow and crisp.

Melissa Freeman (12)
Ecclesbourne School

CRAB

I remain in the sea,
And sometimes come onto the beach,
When it's warm.

I show off my powerful pincers,
As if they are expensive trainers,
When it's warm.

I resemble a rock
And sometimes go under rocks,
When it's warm.

I hide my head,
And go back in the sea,
When it's cold.

Alex Simpson (12)
Ecclesbourne School

THE TRAIN

As fast as a bullet
Speeding past,
Going so fast
Hauling so much,
Smoking so much
Whistling so loud,
As fast as a bullet
Speeding by,
Puffing along
Ever so fast.

Richard Waters (11)
Ecclesbourne School

AUTUMN IS . . .

Autumn is misty and cold
Autumn is rain and frost
Autumn is blue skies with clouds
Autumn is when people wrap up warm
And put fires on
Autumn is children playing in the fallen leaves
Autumn is birds singing on the bare branches
Autumn is conkers falling
Autumn is seeing the stars at night
Autumn is seeing my dad smile
When he unwraps his presents.

Stuart Brocklehurst (12)
Ecclesbourne School

WITCHES BREW

The night is cold, a candle shone,
With every human dead and gone,
Looming together, out they come,
In their heads, torture, pain!
One chanted a spell, a fire appeared,
Into their cauldron, the witches peered.
'Water, water!' one shouted out loud,
The other two knelt, nodded and bowed.
After a while the others came,
Feeling for a fire with a scalding flame.
'Eyes of toad, foxes and wolves,
Blood of humans, brains of fools.
Heart of pig, wing of bat,
Straggly hair and a faithful cat.
Mix it all up as dawn is breaking,
Macbeth your heart will soon be aching!'

Emily Martin (13)
Frederick Gent School

OLYMPICS

An athlete from Britain
Wore a strange mitten,
He played basketball
But was far too small,
And came home with a kitten.

In Atlanta we got one gold
But in Sydney we got eleven,
The athletes seemed as though they were in Heaven
To see their friends bring the medals home,
And the first came in the velodrome.

Mr Chun
Went with a bun,
He saw Mr Redgrave
And his mate Dave,
As England came and won!

Sean Griggs (11)
Frederick Gent School

OLYMPICS

Olympics are boring, Olympics are crap,
What's the point in boxers having a scrap?
To win a gold medal, that's what they try
If they don't, they cry, cry, cry.
The rowers on the boat and they don't win,
If they do then they jump right in.
What's the point in sweating just to get first?
When the folk who come last, they feel the worst.

Luke Brooks (13)
Frederick Gent School

MY DOG

My dog is called Ben,
He is twelve years old,
He is a retriever,
And his fur is gold.

With his big brown eyes,
And his silky ears
It's hard to believe
I've had him for twelve years.

Ben's always been a playful dog,
He gets me out of breath,
Visitors need not fear him,
He'll just lick them half to death.

I know he's had a long life,
And it's got to end in tears,
He'll play at almost anything
But fireworks he fears.

I'll dread the day he leaves me,
They'll never be another,
For Ben means so much to me,
He's more like my big brother.

Rachael Wagstaff (11)
Frederick Gent School

ROW, ROW, ROW YER BOAT

Row, row, row yer boat
hysterically down the Thames.
If yer don't, we'll probably lose
and we'll all cry again.

Nicky James (13)
Frederick Gent School

OLYMPIC POETRY

I'd give a medal to my mum, I don't think I should
I'd give a medal to my dad, I really think I should
I'd give a medal to my fish, he's always in a dish
I'd give a medal to my dog, he's always in a snog
I'd give a medal to my cat, he's always in the mat
I'd give a medal to myself, I'm always in a shelf
I'd give a medal to my friend, he's never on the mend.

Steve Redgrave, Steve Redgrave, I nearly failed the grade
Steve Redgrave, Steve Redgrave, I nearly made the grave
Steve Redgrave, Steve Redgrave, I nearly made a wave
Steve Redgrave, Steve Redgrave, I nearly made a cave
Steve Redgrave, Steve Redgrave, I'm always in a *wave!*

Robert Stevens (11)
Frederick Gent School

I'M AN OLYMPIC RUNNER

I'm an Olympic runner, running is my life.
If someone told me to stop, I'd stab them with a knife.
I run all day, I run all night, even through the rain.
Which my friends and I quite agree, that is quite insane.
Instead of getting on the bus, I run all the way to school.
And even my family think I am a fool.
If I could, I really would, run the speed of light.
Then I could sneak up on my mum and give her a great, big fright.
But now reality, I am in fact not fast.
As slow, in fact, so slow - I always come in last.

Matthew Smart (12)
Frederick Gent School

OLYMPICS (GOLD FOR BOREDOM)

The Olympics bore us rigid,
We pay no attention to it,
But everyone around us,
Thinks we are boring gits.

We really cannot help it,
We don't like sport at all,
It's just a waste of money,
We wish it would just crumble and fall.

Running round the track,
What use is that to us,
Anybody sensible,
Would go and catch the bus.

What a waste of energy,
Just throwing things around,
They jump over high bars,
To just end up on the ground.

Swimmers are very silly,
They obviously have no brain,
They all swim to one end,
Just to come back again.

Gymnasts swing from bar to bar,
What on earth is the point?
They swing like monkeys up a tree,
But they may just break a joint.

So as you all can see,
The Olympics are a bore,
So when it comes round again,
Make it against the *law!*

Bernadette Davies & Charlotte Armiger (12)
Frederick Gent School

MY OLYMPIC POEM

The flame is lit once again
Four whole years we've waited
Sydney in the year 2000
The Olympics have just started!

Many people from afar
Have come to watch the Olympic Games
The competitors would like to win some medals
As the crowds are chanting their names!

Now the crowds are roaring
As the first race has begun
Everyone is running, running
As they are all having fun!

Now it's time to end the games
Many medals have been won
Everyone is going home
It's time to leave the blazing sun!

Jemma Cotterill (12)
Frederick Gent School

DOG RACING

D   is for the tired, *dopey* dogs in the back of the van.
O   is for the *obstacle* laid out with wet sand.
G   is for the *gates* opening wide.
R   is for *racing* around the track.
A   is for *arriving* there and then.
C   is for going fast around the sharp *corners.*
I   is for *inspecting* if the dogs are alright.
N   is for the long, wet, cold, tired *nights.*
G   is for the *gallons* of water the dogs drink.

Hannah Hall (11)
Frederick Gent School

MORRIS GREEN

Morris Green, Morris Green, running down the lane
Morris Green, Morris Green, is going to win again
Morris Green, Morris Green, he has got no lack
Morris Green, Morris Green, is burning down the track
Morris Green, Morris Green, is five foot nine
Morris Green, Morris Green, is a favourite of mine
Morris Green, Morris Green, fastest man in the world
Morris Green, Morris Green, his hair is not curled
Morris Green, Morris Green, is definitely not on the hold
Morris Green, Morris Green, is very much so bald
Morris Green, Morris Green, is a real running machine.

Lewis Marshall (11)
Frederick Gent School

SYDNEY OLYMPICS

S   upporters of the Olympics
Y   oung and old
D   edicated athletes
N   o better we are told
E   veryone in awe
Y   ou could win a gold

O   ld and young people
L   ove it on TV
Y   ears since it started
M   eans so much to me
P   innacle for athletes
I   'd travel far to see
C   alling, 'Go, go, go'
S   o that ends the glee.

Ashley Prentice (12)
Frederick Gent School

THE WIZARD OF MOUNT CRAZY

There is a wizard
Nutty is his name
He is a bit mad
But it was a shame
About 12 years ago
It was the drink that caused the bad luck
He ran out in the road
To stop a speeding Guinness truck
Now he spends his day
Rolling round the floor
Squealing sounds and gabbling
And mixing spells galore
That fall apart
And blow up in his face
How he's called a wizard
It's pretty hard to tell
But it just goes to show
What drink does to you
So next time you see a drop
Flush it down the loo.

Ryan Cannon (12)
Frederick Gent School

OLYMPIC POEM

I would give a gold medal to me sister,
Na! I don't really think I would,
I would give a gold medal to me brother,
Na! I don't really think I could.

I would give a gold medal to me mum,
Na! She always has a scranny at me,
I would give a gold medal to me dad,
Na! He tells me off when I'm having my tea.

I would give a gold medal to me friends,
Na! 'Cos they mess about all the time,
I would give a gold medal to me cousins,
Na! They always want what is mine.

There is only one person I know,
Who deserves all the medals I see,
The bronze, silver and gold medals
Should go to a person like me!

Michelle Charlesworth (14)
Frederick Gent School

OLYMPIC POETRY

I'm the great Olympic writer
I write so easily
On a bus or in a queue
Verses come to me.

I'm the great Olympic writer
I'm always filled with glee
Meeting famous people
Is my speciality.

I'm the great Olympic writer
Seeing people run so free
Sprinting here, sprinting there
Just like a chimpanzee.

I'm the great Olympic writer
Fourteen medals for me
I'm the great Olympic writer
The best in history.

Vickie Yeomans (12)
Frederick Gent School

THE SARAH PAYNE BALLAD

There was a girl playing in a field
Her name was Sarah Payne
Unfortunately this story
Ends tragically with pain.

She fell out with her family
And walked away depressed
She was walking back to her gran's house
And she was found dead and undressed.

Cold and lifeless and all alone
In a cornfield where her body lay
Her life cut short, what a shame
No more laughter or innocent play.

The owner of the land
He couldn't believe his eyes
When he saw a little girl
In front of him she lies.

The police were gathered in their tens
To see what happened to Sarah.

Joe Marriott (12)
Frederick Gent School

OLYMPIC POEM

They thought England's boats were a joke
Until Redgrave to his stroke
The water was cold
But he came back with the gold.

Jonathan Edwards wore great pumps
To do his hop, step and jump.
He landed on his rump
But still did a great, big jump.

Round and round the track
Speed they did not lack
Tried to escape from the pack
But they still pulled back.

The Olympics came to a close
The medal tally had rose
We all stood for a pose
The Olympics finally closed.

Antony Carr (13)
Frederick Gent School

DARK CITY

Everyone in the world should have pity
For the people in the dark city.
People, who by day are normal,
By night are invaded by the paranormal.
Everyone in the world should have pity
For the people in the dark city.

All the sins of mankind gather in the people's minds,
Until, at last, their minds are full,
And they suffer agony, pain and the aching of the skull.
Everyone in the world should have pity
For the people in the dark city.

To balance out the pain and pleasure on the Earth
They have to suffer for others mirth,
But, unfortunately for them their pain is eternal,
For the suffering won't stop as they are immortal.
Everyone in the world should have pity
For the people in the dark city.

Martin Keeling (13)
Frederick Gent School

PETROL BALLAD!

Desperate for the petrol,
The police beg for people to stay away,
The massive line of cars were stuck on
the slipway.

People are in queues,
sitting in the rain,
children are crying,
it's driving them insane.

Police said there was flooding,
On the motorway,
No one listens to them because it was
Tuesday.

The clock was already ticking,
The writing was on the wall,
People looked for tankers,
But none came at all.

The parents were getting desperate,
The children were having a ball,
No schools to be open,
They couldn't believe it all.

Two weeks had passed,
The price of fuel was too high,
So the protesters said,
'Where was Tony Blair?
Lying in his bed.'

The crisis was over,
Will they try again?
Who knows what will happen,
When the workers reign?

Leanne Beaton (12)
Frederick Gent School

CONCORDE CRASH

It was the 27th July when it happened,
People saved up the money to go on,
The Concorde Jet took off
And they were all gone.

People in the jet were finally going to meet New York,
But they didn't know their death was soon.
People inside giggled with joy
And the jet crashed at noon.

The Concorde crashed into a hotel
Crashing up in flames,
The people inside yelled
But the pilot couldn't control it, what a shame.

There were 100 passengers and 9 crew,
Their friends were crying in pain.
The inspectors found a piece of metal and said
'This could happen again!'

As this has happened
All the Concordes have to be checked,
To see if they were alright to fly
But half of them were wrecked.

Their relatives will miss them a lot
Now they're not here
The crash happened a few days ago
It is all becoming too clear.

Yee-Ling Tsang (12)
Frederick Gent School

OLYMPIENS

There's an alien, there's an alien.
Winning all the races
He's not even trying
He's getting all first places.

I saw him in the running
He was oh so very cunning
It was a very good race
He was at a fast pace.

He ended with 17 golds
So I was told
I ended with nothing
He thought I was bluffing.

Ashley Stocks (13)
Frederick Gent School

SYDNEY OLYMPICS

I would give a bronze to my mum
because she feeds me every day.

I would give a silver to my dad
because he takes me to the bay.

I would give a bronze to my teacher
because she once set me a test.

I would give a silver to my mates
because they like to rest.

I would give a gold to me
because I'm just *simply the best!*

Tom Gardom (12)
Frederick Gent School

OLYMPIC GAMES!

O lympics, the very word makes me proud,
L oudly the crowd shouts,
Y elling for the athletes to do their best,
M ore and more gold medals pile on,
P ushing our country nearer the top,
I f only we could get a few more golds,
C ould we actually manage it?

G oing and going, pushing themselves to the limit,
A ll the country is watching on edge of their seats,
M any more get gold, silver and bronze medals,
E ngland gets eleven gold medals,
S oon they come home to their families!

Joanna Robinson (13)
Frederick Gent School

RUNNING RACE

R eady, people waiting to start,
U ntil the track is checked the race can't begin.
N othing can stop the determined runners.
N ight and day the people trained.
I n five minutes the race begins,
N o worries, none at all,
G o, go, go they ran and ran as fast as they could.

R iot in the crowd, cheering and waving.
A ll the runners, panting and sweating.
C hampion to be nearly at the finish,
E nd, he wins the Olympic running race.

Claire Martin (11)
Frederick Gent School

THE OLYMPICS

O rdinary people like you and me,
L ike those in Sydney.
Y oung and old,
M en and women going for gold.
P eople trying their best,
I ntent to prove they're the best, better than the rest,
C ould you do it?

G old, bronze and silver medals,
A   cyclist pushing on his pedals,
M oving slowly and then fast,
E ven though he could be last.
S o still think you can do it?

I magine training for four years,
N o medal guaranteed.

S teve Redgrave has won five,
Y ou haven't even tried.
D eciding to go in the Olympics,
N ever knowing when you'll be picked,
E ven if you tried
Y ou couldn't do it!

Amy Coleman (13)
Frederick Gent School

THE GOLDEN FLAME

The golden flame was very bright,
It lights up the sky on this very night,
All together everybody screamed,
All because of a lovely beam.

The crowds roar just like tigers,
Just to see lots of fires,
Under the sky,
To see lots of different people run by.

People ran and ran until they stopped,
When they got to the end they all dropped,
What a relief it was to be,
At the Olympic Games in Sydney.

Kirsty Renshaw (11)
Frederick Gent School

ARMCHAIR OLYMPICS

I've been training for this for years,
Always wanting to win,
No one knows what I go through,
Waiting for this time to begin.

I pick up the baton,
Ready to start,
I'm in the right place,
I love taking part.

The gun goes *bang,*
I kick off my shoes,
Who's going to win
And who's going to lose?

I get up,
Ready to cheer,
I look at the fridge,
I reach for a beer.

I'm full of excitement,
Ready to drink,
I grab the remote,
In the armchair I sink.

Samantha Riley (13)
Frederick Gent School

OLYMPIC POETRY

I don't like the Olympics,
I don't know any people.
I'd rather stay at home
And listen to heavy metal!

I don't like the Olympics,
I don't think it's exciting.
I'd rather stay at home
And get struck by lightning!

I don't like the Olympics,
I don't think it's a boil.
I'd rather stay at home
And eat silver foil!

I don't like the Olympics,
I think I'd go red.
I'd rather stay at home
And go to bed!

I really don't like the Olympics,
I think I made that clear.
Thank goodness they won't come back
For another four years.

Nikki Ross (11)
Frederick Gent School

HER BROKEN HEART

This is her heart,
And her heart it shall be,
The tears it floods
Fills a blood red sea.

This heart of hers
Is shattered to pieces,
It's like broken glass
But this glass creases.

She's all on her own,
Like in the dark,
She thinks of the past,
When they met in the park.

When she turns,
There is standing
Her ex-boyfriend
Undemanding.

When their eyes meet
They kiss and she tells,
She says 'What's the date
For the wedding bells?'

Cheryl Payne (13)
Frederick Gent School

OLYMPIC PRESSURE

I've tried so hard,
I've run so fast,
My feet thud from the pain,
I just feel as if everyone and everybody counted on me,
They don't know the feeling of defeat,
I do . . .

I'm now so tired,
I'm now so sad,
My head is spinning as I get on my knees and cry,
I just feel as if everyone and everybody counted on me,
They don't know the feeling of defeat,
I do . . .

Sydney sounds so quiet,
But only to me,
The rest are still celebrating for what they've achieved,
I just feel as if everyone and everybody counted on me,
They don't know the feeling of defeat,
I do . . .

So why should I feel this way? I've trained so hard, run so fast,
But still after my best I feel the worst.
Should it have been me cheering with the coach,
Clutching that gold medal?
Winning may not be for me,
Wait, could it be the winner's me? The judges got it wrong,
I'm not the worst, I'm the best, that cheering's now for me!

Amy Ogden (12)
Frederick Gent School

LIFE

Life is like a time bomb
Waiting to explode.
On to your possessions
You must tightly hold.

Love is a mystery
Untouched by all men.
Sleep is a time passer
But tonight I'll sleep again.

Freedom is just a saying,
It never does exist.
A rainbow is just an eye catcher
Before it fades into the mist.

A tear is just a raindrop
Dripping from your face.
Awkward is just a feeling
When you think you're out of place.

The sun is just a fireball
Floating way up high.
Want is when you want something
But you can't get it when you try.

The sky is just an open mass,
It never has an end.
Broke is when it's ruined
Like a broken heart it cannot mend.

Vicki Gibson (13)
Frederick Gent School

THE OLYMPIC STUFF

The five Olympic rings, black, green, yellow, blue and red,
What different records will we get on life ahead.
A lot of sweat in a heap, it doesn't matter if you win or lose you
                                                        still compete.
Our British rowers are excellent, that's because they're confident.
Tomorrow is another day, for the tired runners to run away.
In the mist you can see, something that it is to be.
You can see the Olympic stand, if you shade the sun with your hand.
Never, never will it be that England will win the Olympic gold.

Adam Brown (13)
Frederick Gent School

OLYMPICS

O lympics is a game of sports,
L ots and lots of different sorts,
Y ear 2000 is the year,
M edals are to be worn here,
P eople running round the track,
I   n 1st, 2nd and 3rd they come,
C elebrations were happening everywhere,
S ydney is where the Olympics were held!

Shaun Castledine (14)
Frederick Gent School

THE BALLAD OF MARY AND JODIE

Mary and Jodie were born on August the 8th,
Joined together by the tummy,
Sharing a heart and a pair of lungs,
But they each have their own dummy!

Jodie is bright and healthy,
Mary has a deformed face,
She lives off Jodie,
This is a serious case!

Judge Justice Johnson rules the court,
Deciding the fate of the girls,
He orders the surgeons to separate the twins,
Their lives to be unfurled.

The parents say 'It's God's will that both should die,'
The doctors had no interest with what they said,
The appeal still continues,
While the two poor babies lie in bed.

The pro-life said they're not in agreement,
They think they should stay together,
As this is the way they were born,
They will breathe as one forever.

The Roman Catholic leader wrote to the court,
He also disagrees to their separation,
The doctors say that both girls will die,
The issue is one of desperation.

The court has decided,
The parents have agreed,
Mary's life is over,
The operation will proceed.

Marc Faulder (12)
Frederick Gent School

OLYMPIC POEM!

Fireworks are jumping out sparkling over me,
I'm trying to count them as fast as I can 1, 2, 3.

The Olympic rings are shining bright, circular and gold,
The rings have been lit up tonight, all tickets are sold.
The athletes are on the track ready to compete.
They're running as fast as they can, burning off some fat.
Sweating like a pig, breathing like a cow,
It will be worth it bowing on the podium.

Corie Brewster (13)
Frederick Gent School

BILLY BOB

I have a little dog
His name is Billy Bob
So glad it's not a frog
Cos I love my Billy Bob.
Billy Bob lets go for a walk,
Find your lead then we'll talk.
About cats, bones and treats
About walking to heel
Next to my feet.
About chasing birds,
Barking at strangers,
Barking to protect me
from Imminent dangers.
Billy Bob what would I do
To not have a dog
As faithful as you.

Robert Bradley (11)
Glossopdale Community College

A Shimmering Seasons Lake

A spring lake soft and special,
Ringlets stirring the lake from its deep sleep
Like a hedgehog waking from hibernation,
Happy as newborn ducklings glide across its smooth surface.

A summer's lake shining and clean,
Reflecting the trees and every thing around
Like a mirror glistening in the sun.
Clear as crystal, smooth as silk.

An autumn lake shimmering and deep,
Leaves fall from trees
Like baby birds learning to fly,
The clear blue sky making the water look like ice.

A winter lake cold and clear,
Lonely as the birds fly south
Like a single cloud in the sky,
Reflecting the moon on its cold, icy surface,
Shimmering and gleaming as the winter comes to an end.

Heather Parry (11)
Glossopdale Community College

Autumn And Winter

Autumn comes once a year bringing,
Bare trees, everywhere crispy,
Crunchy leaves crackle when you stand on them,
Brown, yellow and red, the colour of autumn leaves.
Becoming cold it turns to winter,
Glistening snow drops on trees,
Merry people having fun sledging in the snow,
Days get brighter and longer as it turns to spring.

Susan Townley (11)
Glossopdale Community College

LIFE ON MARS

Life on Mars will never be the same again,
But aliens will remain,
But aliens will remain,
My mission to Mars was hectic,
And because there was no gravity I spun around and cut my
Head on one of the door handles and my head went septic.

Life on Mars will never be the same again,
But aliens will remain,
But aliens will remain,
Mars was red,
But the aliens were green,
But the aliens were green.

When I left I didn't feel the same,
I felt sad to leave the aliens up on the planet of Mars.

Life on Mars will never be the same again,
But aliens will remain,
But aliens will remain.

Victoria Barlow (11)
Glossopdale Community College

THE DOG NEXT DOOR!

It started the day the neighbours went
To buy a little pup,
It turned out to be a giant one,
And really big and *tough.*

I thought that I could handle it
Barking in the night,
But what this beast was asking for
Was a flipping great big fight.

I told the next-door neighbours
Why I couldn't sleep,
They said that they were sorry
To bother all the street.

So now that that's all sorted
I'll try and get some rest,
I'll be lucky if I manage
But I'll try my very best.

Kate Gatley (11)
Glossopdale Community College

A JOURNEY TO MARSHMALLOW LAND

It all started after I'd eaten a huge bag of marshmallows
I looked at my tank to find my fish floating down in the shallows
I thought oh dear, oh what a shame
Now which fish food should I blame
I laid down sprawled out on my bed
What had made my poor fish dead.

When I opened my eyes I was amazed to see
A big pink marshmallow staring at me
I rubbed my eyes again and again
Until I felt quite a hurtful pain
I ate all that I could see
A marshmallow cat a part of me
And then I woke up in my bed
I looked at my poor fish (still dead)
I said 'Oh dear, it was me
I gave it a marshmallow for its tea.'

Tim Nudds (11)
Glossopdale Community College

STORM OF DISASTERS

On the night of Christmas Eve the storm that brought disasters started,
Lights went out, people began to worry, they blamed it on the weather.
Snow was a blizzard, thunder was a drum,
Lightning was a shock for each and everyone.
Rain battered down upon the sheltered homes,
Babies began to cry, faces full of groans.
Then there was silence, not a word was spoken,
People walked outside to see if the storm had broken.
The clouds were white, the rain had stopped,
The thunder had gone but the lightning had not.
Then out of a dream not another word was made,
Houses seemed quiet, everyone was afraid.

Valentina Wood (11)
Glossopdale Community College

FUTURISTIC EVENTS

The future is out there . . .
Where the planets are islands
And spaceships whiz and whirl,
The Milky Way long and elegant.

The future is out there . . .

Where the cries of help are unheard
As you float and float forever,
Pluto, Uranus and Mars inhabited like the Earth,
The black holes swallow their prey like hungry tigers.

The future is out there . . .

Jack Haworth (12)
Glossopdale Community College

STORM ON THE OCEAN

We were in the middle of a sea of silk, black clouds were
                                        brewing ahead.
Nothing else mattered to me apart from getting to where we said.
As soon as the waves crashed against the rocks and I saw the birds
                                       flying back from sea,
I had a feeling of sudden pain, or was it a sad memory?
Then the rain started and I had a vision of fear.
The thought was so strong that happy moments began to disappear.
All day long and all night through, tragedy was in my mind.
Would I see my family again? Would my life rewind?
I thought about my mother and father.
I thought about my friends.
I thought about the pouring rain.
Would it ever end?

Anna Pickard (11)
Glossopdale Community College

THE JOURNEY INTO SLEEPLAND

As I close my eyes I wonder,
I wonder what my imagination thinks at night.

I wonder, I wonder,
How long does it take me to finally
Drift off to Sleepland?

I wonder, I wonder,
What nonsense will I think about tonight?
What will I dream about tonight?

And then it is all over . . .
I am fast asleep in Sleepland.

Christopher James (11)
Glossopdale Community College

I WISH

I wish I was a wizard
To cast some magic spells
To click my fingers and end up on Mars
To walk one step to a thousand yards.

I wish I was a sunbeam
High up in the sky
Bursting with colour shining bright
Cast on the world with amazing light.

I wish I was a flower
Standing in full bloom
Attracting butterflies, insects and bees
Drifting and turning towards the sun with ease.

Helen Cant (11)
Glossopdale Community College

I SAW A DOG IN THE STARRY SKY!

I saw the dog in the starry sky.
I saw the moon wave goodbye.
I saw a child wetting the rocks.
I saw a wave in the box.
I saw the toys scream and shout.
I saw a madman starving in the drought.
I saw a boy swallow a boat.
I saw a whale wearing a coat.
I saw a woman made of bricks.
I saw a house eat a Twix.
I saw a girl that lives on Saturn.
I saw a man that saw this happen.

Natalie Simpson (11)
Heanor Gate School

THERE IS A BOY

There is a boy in our class
Who can't concentrate on English or maths,
They say something happened;
A problem at home,
His mother left him, he feels so alone.
Now he feels he can't go on,
People try to convince him,
He can't go on.

There is a boy,
Who spends his time,
Gazing up at the clock, waiting for it to chime,
He hasn't any friends,
He says he doesn't want them,
He doesn't need them now.

There is a boy,
Who dreams of the day,
When he could hear his father say,
Don't worry son it's OK!

Laura Bexson (11)
Heanor Gate School

I SAW A MAN SCUTTLE ACROSS THE FLOOR

I saw a man scuttle across the floor.
I saw a mouse chase a wild boar.
I saw a wolf make a car.
I saw a builder trapped in a jar.
I saw a bug totally explode.
I saw a building crack a code.
I saw a spy covered with nits.
I saw some hair, 'I'm falling to bits.'

Richard Wilcoxson (12)
Heanor Gate School

I SAW AN ELEPHANT FLYING HIGH

I saw an elephant flying high.
I saw a pigeon in a starry sky.
I saw a moon jump and shout.
I saw a child fly about.
I saw a spaceship hurt a boy.
I saw a madman with a Barbie toy.
I saw a girl sail on the sea.
I saw a ship stare at me.
I saw a mouse strict and mean.
I saw a teacher thin and lean.
I saw a lady broken and bent.
I saw a chair that paid no rent.
I saw a tramp with fluffy clouds.
I saw a sky that was very proud.
I saw a king with a superhero.
I saw a film called 'Spearow'.
I saw a Pokémon with an end.
I saw a poem twist and bend.
I saw a wing with a banana.
I saw a monkey eating sultanas.
I saw these things and that is plain
But now I am probably insane.

David Rayner (11)
Heanor Gate School

THE LONELY FISH!

I was a fish all alone in the sea,
Not a friend in the world has poor old me,
I swim in the sea
Dreaming of all the good times there could be
If only I had a friend,
Poor me.
I've spent my life alone as can be,
No one there to comfort me,
No one wants me around in the sea
So I wait for a fishing boat to pass by
I wait and wait,
Sigh and sigh.
Yahoo! Whoopee!
Fishing boat for me
They throw down a net
I swim right in
Get taken aboard
Get put in a tin.
'Oh look how sweet'
Cries someone grim,
I must take it to show my best friend Tim.
Now here I am sitting in a bowl
With a lonely heart and a waiting soul.

Sunny Saini (12)
Heanor Gate School

I Saw The Moon Say Sorry Politely

I saw a teenager / shining brightly
I saw the moon / say sorry politely
I saw an e-mail / eat a bag of sweets
I saw a girl / with a beak
I saw a duck / driving a van
I saw a man / eating a can
I saw a dustbin truck / stroking a cat
I saw a lad / come from a hat
I saw a rabbit / dance and sing
I saw a singer / disappear going *ping!*
I saw a magician / fall from space
I saw a meteor / dress in disgrace.

If you don't believe it
Ask the man who saw it with me.

Nickita Allen (12)
Heanor Gate School

I Saw Frankenstein In The Sky

I saw Frankenstein in the sky.
I saw a cloud eating a pie.
I saw a man ready to pounce.
I saw a tiger that weighed an ounce.
I saw a mouse crossing the road.
I saw a schoolboy eating a toad.
I saw a crocodile in bed.
I saw a sick boy who lost his head.
I know that all of this is true
And now we've passed it on to you.

Emily Reston (12)
Heanor Gate School

I Saw A Dog Pouncing On A Mouse

I saw a dog pouncing on a mouse
I saw a cat blow up his house
I saw a man clean his belly
I saw a dog watching telly
I saw a lady in her hole
I saw a mouse on a pole
I saw a bird eating honey
I saw a bee being funny
I saw a clown playing alone
I saw a boy eating a bone
I saw a dog carrying a log
I saw a man sucking a frog
I saw a cat digging in mud
If you do not believe me, look yourselves.

Charlotte Smith (11)
Heanor Gate School

I Saw An Alien Glistening In The Sky!

I saw an alien glistening in the sky
I saw the moon shooting by
I saw a star swallow a shark
I saw a goldfish swinging in the park
I saw a mad man with a curly tail
I saw a pig spit out curly kale
I saw a child laying eggs
I saw a chicken that drinks tea dregs
I saw a cat that lives on Saturn
I saw the girl that watched this happen.

Mark James (11)
Heanor Gate School

I SAW A VISION FIRM AND TALL

I saw a vision firm and tall
I saw a house creeping round a mall
I saw an assassin eat a boat
I saw a whale sleepily gloat
I saw an otter score a goal
I saw a footballer drink out of a bowl
I saw a dog eat a fly
I saw a spider score a try
I saw a rugby star drink cyanide
I saw a mental man do the attack bide
I saw a policeman do the splits
I saw a dancer eat ice-cream sticks
I saw a woodworm jump out of a plane
I saw a skydiver with a hairy mane
I saw a lion in the windowpane
I saw a face I must be insane.

Nigel Wright (11)
Heanor Gate School

I SAW A LITTLE GIRL SHINING IN THE SKY

I saw a little girl shining in the sky
I saw the sun flying by, way up high
I saw a bird looking bright white
I saw a cloud shining in the night
I saw a star in the day
I saw a plane one night in May
I saw the moon eating a pie
I saw a little girl shining in the sky.

Emma-Leigh Flatt (11)
Heanor Gate School

I Saw A Cloud In The Morning Sky

I saw a cloud in the morning sky
I saw the sun jumping high
I saw a dog singing loud
I saw a bird looking proud
I saw a child flying a spaceship
I saw an alien eating a bag of chips
I saw a madman swallow a boat
I saw a whale wearing a denim coat
I saw a woman mooing around
I saw a cow flying up and down
I saw a comet cleaning his truck
I saw a father bringing luck
I saw the moon with six little legs
I saw a granny blue and angry
I saw a sea juicy and tangy
I saw the clouds in the morning sky.

Emily Nightingale (11)
Heanor Gate School

My Dog!

The keeper of the house
Just about to chase a mouse.
Turning round like a flash
Mouse had gone and so has dog
My dog the best of the lot
Barking like a teapot
Howling like the wind
Standing like a petal
Next to a nettle.
My dog!

Isobel Shaw (11)
Heanor Gate School

I Saw A Penguin In A Tree

I saw a penguin in a tree, swim in the sea
I saw a bird fly through space
I saw a comet with top hat and case
I saw a man speed at 90mph
I saw a car sit on a flower
I saw a mouse swallow a man
I saw a T-rex in Sudan
I saw a plane under the water
I saw a fish set in mortar
I saw a statue run away
I saw a cheetah hop for a day
I saw a frog in a stew
I saw these things, they all are true,
But if you agree no one will believe you.

Ben Wain (11)
Heanor Gate School

I Saw An Old Man Swimming In The Sea!

I saw an old man swimming in the sea
I saw a whale sitting down for tea
I saw a family being blown up
I saw a balloon drinking from a cup
I saw a baby waving in the breeze
I saw a tree begging on his knees
I saw a servant cooking on a pan
I saw a sausage driving in a van
I saw an old man swimming in the sea
I saw a whale looking at me.

Danielle Manson (12)
Heanor Gate School

I Saw A Dress Flapping Its Wings!

I saw a dress flapping its wings
I saw a bird plucking its strings
I saw a guitar in the sky
I saw a star trying to fly
I saw a baby bird go speeding past
I saw a car running fast
I saw a dog biting his cage
I saw a hamster get in a rage
I saw a madman go into a hole
I saw a mouse in the North Pole
I saw Santa biting his nails
I saw a grandad playing with its tail
I saw a cat doing the splits
I saw a girl falling to bits.

Jessica Briggs (11)
Heanor Gate School

I Saw A Pig Eating A Mouse

I saw a pig eating a mouse,
I saw a cat in a house,
I saw a man speaking to God,
I saw a church playing with a dog
I saw a witch in a glittery night
I saw the moon having a fight
I saw a boy with black and white stripes
I saw a zebra wiping her mouth
I saw a girl going south
I saw a pig eating a mouse.

Emma Hall (11)
Heanor Gate School

I Saw A Barbie Floating In The Air

I saw a Barbie floating in the air
I saw a cloud in the shape of a bear
I saw a bush roar like mad
I saw a lion hugging his dad
I saw a boy burn down in flames
I saw a house marry a dame
I saw an old man having a perm
I saw a lady eating worms
I saw a bird do a somersault
I saw a gymnast fixing a bolt
I saw a workman teach maths
I saw a teacher doing a plaster cast
I saw a nurse spin a ball on her nose
I saw a seal step into a sunbed
I saw a model making herself look dead
I saw a movie star snap a pencil lead
I saw a student deliver a letter
I saw a postman making his work better
I saw a schoolboy in a box
I saw a lipstick go to sleep
If you don't believe me have a peep!

Chloe Deng (11)
Heanor Gate School

MY BISCUIT

It's crumbly
It's crunchy
It's as golden as wheat
It's criss crossed back is mouth-watering
The sweet smell of beautiful biscuit
The sugar sparkles like crystals
It leaves a trail of appetising crumbs.

Joe Redfern (12)
Highfields School

TEN THINGS FOUND IN A LOST ASTRONAUT'S POCKET

1 a shooting star
2 a severed alien head
3 a control stick
4 a bottle of vodka
5 a photo of himself
6 a compact mirror
7 a spare head
8 a hair brush
9 styling gel
10 a chicken vindaloo

Nathan Wheeler (12)
Highfields School

HATE

Hate is red
It smells of death
It sounds like screams of pain

It tastes like blood
It looks like war
Hate overwhelms me

Hate is bad
Hate is evil
Hate kills too many people.

Peter Wildgoose (12)
Highfields School

IN MUM'S POCKET

In Mum's pocket there is
A dummy or two
A nappy with poo
A bunch of keys
A hanky of sneeze
The babies' tea
A picture of *he*
A glass eye
A piece of pie
A headache pill
Her dad's will.

Sam Brownlee (12)
Highfields School

APRIL FOOLS!

'Mum! Mum! dad's dropped the chainsaw!'
'Ha! Ha! Got ya! April Fools!'

'Dad! Dad! Mum's dyed her hair *pink*!'
'Ha! Ha! Got ya April Fools!'

'Jackie! Jackie! Andrew your boyfriend's gone missing!'
'Ha! Ha! Got ya! April Fools!'

Oh no! It's ten o'clock April Fools is over.
No more pranks. No more tricks!

'Ryan! Ryan! Watch out that ladder is going to fall on you!'

'Ha, Ha very funny. April Fools is over!'

'No seriously it's going to . . .'

Crash!

Claire Gamble (12)
Newbold Community School

THE DIFFICULT POEM

You wouldn't believe I could be so stressed
Writing a poem is a pest
How can I win
With a brain like a bin?
Full of rubbish and stupid ideas
If you were like this you'd be in tears
But I'm going to get it right
Even if I have to stay up all night
I'll even write it bit by bit,
Hey I've written a poem, without knowing it.

Amy Scott (12)
Newbold Community School

MY HORRID PET BOGEY

My pet bogey is horrid and slimy
You don't have a pet bogey I bet.

Hates all my friends, so it does but maybe that's because they hate him.
Orange and green is the colour of it.
Runny and slimy or you could say
Runny and sick
It climbs up walls and sticks to the TV
Dipsy and stupid so it is.

Picky eater so it is
Eat it if you dare.
Tomorrow I might sell it to you.

Bogey can do lots of tricks
Open doors
Greet people
Get up people's noses and
Eat little bogeys but
Yesterday I picked it out of my nose
So it's well trained for a day old.

Matthew Woodward (11)
Newbold Community School

WINTER

In winter it rains,
In winter it's cold,
In winter it snows
In winter all the little children build snowmen.

In winter it's icy,
In winter it's foggy,
In winter sleet falls from the sky,
In winter all the little children build snowmen.

In winter it's windy,
In winter it gales,
In winter it's frosty,
In winter all the little children build snowmen.

Toni Jacques (12)
Newbold Community School

IT'S JUST LOVE

This feeling just won't part
It's the colour that's oh so bright
It's from the depths of my heart
And it definitely isn't cream or white.

It's my burning desire
It's just like a fire.
It's my burning desire
It's just like a fire.

The flames are there
People stop and stare.
It feels like they can see right through me
But how can they see.

It's my burning desire
It's just like a fire
It's my burning desire
It's just like a fire.

When it all goes dark
This makes the mark
That love's so strong
And lasts to long.

Tara Hutton (12)
Newbold Community School

TY BEANIES

TY is the name for me
They're all my beanies for all to see.

There's Spangles, Kicks and Diana too
There's even Ariel and lots more that's new

Blue, green, red and white
There's so many colours, for your delight

Beanies, bears, kids and buddies too
Not to forget the animals, it's like a zoo.

Beanie bears are so cool
I love them all, they certainly rule

Stars and stripes, Fuzz and Luke
They're all my favourites, which ones for you

2000 Signature is a special bear
This is because it's colours are purple and red
It's TY tag is on it's ear
It hangs so brightly never to disappear.

Louise Lukic (12)
Newbold Community School

LOVE

Love is blind - blind as a bat
No one knowing what you feel
It's like a mouse getting past a big cat
But your heart is sealed.

Butterflies are flying around
Your trying to keep it in
As your heart pounds
When you stare in the wilderness.

And you think
You're the key to my heart
You make me feel pink
You're the only thing I see

Love is blind - blind as a bat
No one knowing what you feel
It's like a mouse getting past a big cat
But your heart is sealed.

Michelle Batteson (12)
Newbold Community School

THE EMPTY WILDERNESS

There, where I stood.
I stood still, out there I looked.
I looked out to the empty wilderness.
The empty wilderness was still.
Still as anything I stood.
I stood and watched the sun go down.
Down went the sun and into the horizon.
The horizon was brighter than ever.
Brighter than ever I had seen.
I had seen it go down many times before.
Before I could say anything it had gone.
Gone darker than the last time.
Time had passed.
Passed before my eyes.
My eyes blurred.
Blurred to darkness.
Darkness had fallen.
Fallen to where I stood.

Emma Bramall (12)
Newbold Community School

I HATE SCHOOL

School, school, I hate school
All my friends think I'm a fool
because *I hate school!*
All you hear all day long
Is 'don't do that' and 'that's all wrong!'
All teachers say is 'Mend your ways.'
Whilst walking down the corridor their eyes ablaze
Like . . . yesterday I ripped a page out of my book.
The teacher came over and everyone stared and looked
I only wanted to tell my friend the joke about the lorry
and now I've got to stay behind and say I'm sorry.
All that for a joke that wasn't funny!
School, school, I hate school
All my friends think I'm a fool
Because *I hate school!*

Emma Clark (13)
Newbold Community School

THE DOG DOWN THE ROAD

The dog down the road I hate so
It's not very nice and it has some lice
It barks all day, it barks all night
It really does give me a fright.
Its teeth are sharp and white
It has got a terrible bite.
Once it acted cute and cuddly
A man went to stroke it but blew it
It bit his arm chewed and pulled
It pulled him down, took him out
So don't be fooled by little Chihuahuas
Or you might lose an arm or two.

Mark Barnett (12)
Newbold Community School

ALL ABOUT MY DOG CALLED CASSIE

I like to have a lark
At Holmbrook Valley Park
I like to have a stick
And give my mum a lick.

I see another dog called Cassie
But I dread to see a dog called Lassie
I like to get very muddy
And I've got two friends called Gunner and Sunny.

My pack leader is just called Andy
And when I go to Wales I get very sandy.
I think you've heard most of my poem I'd just like to say
My name is Cassie Milroy and I like a good play!

Oliver Milroy (12)
Newbold Community School

CONKERS!

You see the conkers on the tree,
but the conkers can't see me,
you play the game
and then fame the name,
you hear a hit,
that makes a split,
taste the conker,
taste the tree,
they seem the
same to me,
they feel smooth,
but not with a groove,
it doesn't smell like my tea,
it smells like a tree.

Helen Anne Lawrie (11)
Newbold Community School

CHRISTMAS POEM

Every Christmas, under my tree,
I find tons of presents of luxury.

But there are children, who aren't so lucky,
Who's clothes are ragged and rather mucky.

Their streets are not full of Christmas cheer,
And they get the same every year.

And every year their only hope,
Is that they can get something, even if it is just a bar of soap,

So you have to ask yourself in despair,
Do you count yourself, lucky not to live there,

So when you get up on Christmas morning,
And come down the stairs tired and yawning,

Just think of all those unfortunate youngsters,
Who could hopefully, one day be amongst us.

Kathryn Ryalls (12)
Newbold Community School

FOOTIE POEM

Football is a brilliant game
But most players come off in pain
There are stars in football
And I'm going to tell you them all

There is Ronald and Frank the De Boer twins
And Rivaldo who plays for the wins
Patrick Kluivert loves to score
And Kanu's amazing skill will never bore

Michael Owen is the main man
And France have got Zinedine Zidane
Roberto Carlos curls free kicks
And Luis Figo does flicks

David Beckham is also good at free kicks
And Raul Gonzalez likes to do tricks
Jaap Stam is strong at the back
And Del Piero is good on the attack

Football is *brilliant.*

Jordan Tunnicliffe (12)
Newbold Community School

ALACA ALACA ZAM ABOUT ME

Alaca alaca zam I really love magic
Alaca alaca zam I wish there was no school
Alaca alaca zam I support Leeds U
Alaca alaca zam I really hate Man U
Alaca alaca zam I like to read Harry Potter
Alaca alaca zam I don't like going to bed
Alaca alaca zam I've got a Time computer
Alaca alaca zam I am always on the Internet
Alaca alaca zam I am always on the PlayStation
Alaca alaca zam I like to watch wrestling
Alaca alaca zam Stone Cold is the best
Alaca alaca zam I've got a brother called Ryan
Alaca alaca zam I like to beat him up
Alaca alaca zam I love every sport
Alaca alaca zam I like riding my bike
Alaca alaca zam I play midfield for Manor Rangers
Alaca alaca zam I'm going to shut up now.

Scott Bollands (11)
Newbold Community School

WHAT A DECISION!

Lollipops and pick n mix
Lion bars and crunchy Twix,
What a decision I have to make,
Please help me for goodness sake.

Can't decide what to eat,
I just know I need a treat.
What a decision I have to make,
Please help me for goodness sake.

Cheese and onion and salt and vinegar frisps
Roast chicken or smoky bacon crisps,
What a decision I have to make
Please help me for goodness sake

Cola, lemonade all these fizzy pops
Please help me decide which one is the tops?
What a decision I have to make,
Please help me for goodness sake.

Perhaps still orange is the best.
I wish I could put them all to the test
What a decision I have to make
Please help me for goodness sake.

If only I could buy them all
Then I could have a ball
What a decision I have to make
Please help me for goodness sake.

Sara Bannister (12)
Newbold Community School

BROTHERS

Brothers can be really annoying
Brothers are a pain in the backside
Brothers are always stabbing you in the back
Brothers are always talking about going in the army
Brothers are after girls
They just can't leave the house without a fight.
Brothers are sometimes kind
Brothers are always getting new things
Brothers are always hogging the computer
Brothers are usually out of the house.

Ben Graham (13)
Newbold Community School

ESCAPE TO WROXHAM

I'm going on holiday in a week
I hope the weather won't be bleak
If there's a flood
I'll need a hood
Or I could use my yella
Umbrella
We're going to Wroxham
And we'll have fun
We'll be on a houseboat
Carrying a coat
I'll bring you a gift
Unless there's a snowdrift
While we're away
We may even come back one day.

Lucy Chadburn (12)
Newbold Community School

CHOCOLATE DREAM

Chocolate is my favourite food
Wherever I am, whatever my mood.
Bars and boxes, packets or bags
A great big box of chocolate fags.
Dairy Milk or Walnut Whips,
Chocolate buttons or chocolate dips
Coffee creams and hazelnut whirls
Specially made for all us girls
When I close my eyes at night
I don't count sheep it's Turkish delight
I go to sleep and in my dreams
Are toffee crisp and strawberry creams
Wherever I am whatever my mood
Chocolate is my favourite food.

Lisa Wilson (12)
Newbold Community School

THE SPARROW

See the sparrow in the tree,
Is he looking down at me?
I stand quite still as not to scare,
I'm quite sure he knows I'm there.

He starts to whistle a merry tune,
He sounds so happy, not full of gloom.
He sits a while to preen his feathers,
They need to be clean in all kinds of weather.

Here's his mate, it's time to go,
No fancy moving, no flying slow.
Goodbye sparrow, have your fun,
I'm sure he will, here comes the sun!

Toni Glover (11)
Newbold Community School

GIRAFFE

Giraffe, giraffe as tall as can be
Giraffe, giraffe what can you see?
Your head so high up in the sky
You're so tall, why, why, why?
Your legs are so long and your neck is too
I wish I could be just like you.

Nice soft skin, yellow and brown
Nice big spots all the way down.
King of the jungle you might not be
Best of them all you are to me.

James Wootton (11)
Newbold Community School

SOFT NIGHTS

Long summer days
Golden with sun
Like dew in the morning
Soon will be gone.
Warm golden moonlight
Shadows black on the grass
Like frost in the morning
All these will pass.

Darker misty nights
Cold with sorrow
Waken in the morning
Vanished tomorrow.
Sleeping softly without a sound
In our hammocks above the ground
Tucked up fast on
Darkness in the morning has all gone.

Alexandria Smith (12)
Newbold Community School

GUESS WHAT?

I'm gonna give you some clues,
Which animal it is you have to choose.

They think of wonderful things,
I like to watch them whilst I sit on the swings.

They don't talk, they just miaow,
But still it tells us how.

How they're feeling happy or sad,
Or if they have done something really bad.

They like to curl up in warm places,
And clean their paws and their faces.

Mine likes to sit on the boiler,
When the weather starts to get cooler.

It also likes to sit in front of the fire,
Whilst quietly chewing on a piece of wire,
Can you guess what it is?

OK I will give you some clues,
Before you finally choose.

Some of you might already know,
But don't worry there's not much more to go.

Of course I know what it is,
But I will describe it a bit.

It has pointy ears,
But it has no fears.

It jumps on tables, climbs on chairs,
Everywhere ginger-white hairs.

It chases mouses,
Out of our houses.

Have you guessed what it is?
Of course you have it is this!

Charlotte Hinde (12)
Newbold Community School

SEASONS

Spring:
Spring brings new life
Daffodils begin to open their petals
Lambs start to graze the meadows
As young birds chirp in their nests.

Summer:
The hot sun shone down
On sweet, little children playing on the beach
Their smiles so big it reaches from ear to ear
Eyes twinkled with happiness.

Autumn:
Leaves fall on the ground
Making trees look bare
Swirling round and round
Like a naked flame.

Winter:
Snow falls slowly and gracefully
Merry children make snowmen in the garden
Christmas lights make houses look like a starry sky
Fireworks shoot up in the air to celebrate the birth of Jesus.

Laura Baldwin (11)
Newbold Community School

DUSK TILL DAWN

I run towards the river
I can smell the bog myrtle as I push through the bushes
Smell of mint lingers in the air
The water's close by.
I reach the river just as dusk wraps the land in mystery
The rocks are slippery and the water's deep
I wait until the sun has gone down
Now the sky is red like blood.
Fish rise to catch the last of the dancing flies
Deer step out of the wood to drink at the river
Maybe an old, grey wolf follows behind.
Watch where the evening star will rise
Mark where the sun goes down.

Deer scatter as I stand
The dark is thicker now
River plants, cold under my feet
Give off a good clean scent.
I run under the yew trees
The dark is all around me now.

Rebecca Taylor (12)
Newbold Community School

FRIENDS

Friends are friendly
Friends are kind
Friends are something
You get along with all the time.

Friends are understanding
Friends are caring
Friends are there for you
When you are feeling down.

Friends aren't selfish
Friends aren't spiteful
Friends aren't something
That you hang around with just sometimes.

Friends aren't bossy
Friends aren't nasty
Friends are something
Everyone needs in their lives.

Emma Ashmore (12)
Newbold Community School

UNDER THE SEA

Under the deep blue sea the sand was soft on my feet
Seaweed tickling my toes, slimy and green
The shimmering shoal of fish swimming all around me
The dolphins calling out to each other
Looking for their mother
Coral waving side to side

Under the deep blue sea oysters having a race
This underwater planet is nothing like space
In a deep dark cave I could only see eyes
Clear white eyes just staring back at me
I took a few steps back and looked around
And then a line of tiny sea horses came out of a mound

Under the deep blue sea I saw a crab and a lobster claw to claw
I want to stay down here forever more
Then I saw a grey pointed fin
And a yellowish wide grin
I swam as quickly as I could to the surface for air
That gave me a great, big scare
I don't think I'll go back down there until, erm, oh tomorrow.

Amie Smith (12)
Newbold Community School

IN TEACHERS POCKETS

Have you ever looked in teachers pockets?
Mouldy tissues and silver lockets,
Old test papers from terms ago.
Pencils and sharpeners that children throw,
Detention slips they like to give out,
To make the children put on a pout.

Have you ever looked in teachers pockets?
Mouldy tissues and silver lockets,
Cooking recipes, the old school mag.
Enough to fit in my school bag,
Lip balm, shoe polish, some chocolate Roses,
The old school photograph with children's poses.

Don't ever look in teachers pockets,
You will find they have no locket.
Just detention slips they like to give out,
To make you put on a pout!

Alison Christian (11)
Newbold Community School

SNOW DAY

It's snowing outside
And the kids are inside.
They long to play out
To scream and to shout.
They put on their coats
To slide down the slopes.
They start a snowball fight
And they get everyone in sight.
They go home to get warm
To get out of the snowstorm.

Allen Pickering (11)
Newbold Community School

ANIMALS

I like animals especially snails
Small and slimy without a tail.
I've got hamsters in my garden shed
One's called Sebastian and one called Fred.

I like dogs less than cats
Because they are big and eat and chase cats.
I've got a lizard, with a long, long tail
It's a green one who likes to eat snails!

Arran Lange (12)
Newbold Community School

THE CABBAGE IS A FUNNY VEG

The cabbage is a funny veg,
All crisp and green and brainy.
I sometimes wear one on my head,
When it's cold and rainy.
When it's cold and rainy,
It's like flakes in space.

Kingsley Davies (11)
Newbold Community School

SPORT

S   wimming is great when it is really hot,
P   otting the balls at snooker with a good shot,
O   llying the ramps on a skateboard,
R   eeves scored a goal and the crowd roared,
T   o play basketball it helps to be tall,
S   port is fun and good for all.

Ben Stacey (12)
Newbold Community School

FRIENDS

Friends should be trustworthy
And care for one another.
Friends should always lend a hand,
Friends should be considerate
And don't bully another friend.
Stick up for a friend when they are in trouble,
Never walk away from a friend
When they need you the most.
Never let a friend down,
Friends are like plants,
If you don't care for them,
They will die.
Be friends forever.

Emma Bradshaw (12)
Newbold Community School

THE OWL

All is quiet on this dark night
As the owl begins its hungry flight.
Looking for food, possibly rats
Joined in the search by scary cats.

Tu-Whit Tu-Whoo and one big swoop
The owl catches a rat, one of a troop.
No one hears and no one sees
As the owl disappears into the trees.

The sun comes up, a new day is here
The owl is asleep with nothing to fear.
High in the treetops, out of harms way
Awaiting another night to hunt for its prey.

Scott Thomas (12)
Newbold Community School

A SPIKEY SURPRISE

My mum wouldn't let,
Me keep another pet,
She got in a huff,
And said the cat was enough,
Even when the cat tray was overflowing,
She still went without knowing,
About my friend Spike.
Though he did like,
To roam through the house,
And chase our resident mouse,
I think he learned that off the cat,
Though I am not too sure about that.
When we went on our holiday,
He did like to lay,
On a stone,
Near our new home.
But one day,
Spike ran away,
I did look,
In every nook,
I looked around,
Then he was found.
When my mum gently placed her rear,
On a stone near here,
And her head,
Went beetroot red,
Though Mum was mad,
I was rather glad,
That Spike was finally back home.

Donna Hoskin (12)
Newbold Community School

Di Canio!

Excitement, excitement all around,
Paolo di Canio's coming to town.
When he puts on the blue and white,
Sheffield Wednesday will do all right.

The fans all loved to chant his name,
Which brought Di Canio record fame.
Before each game they played his tune,
Which sent the crowd over the moon!

Fourteen goals he scored last season,
But the referees had seen him.
Ten yellows seemed a bit hard,
But even worse was the one red card.

This gave Paolo a bad reputation,
Which soon spread around the nation.
Tension arose about his teamwork,
So problems soon began to lurk.

The final straw was the Arsenal game,
Though at first the incident was rather tame.
Viera and Jonk had a childish tussle,
Before our Paolo decided to use his muscle.

Red cards to Paolo and Keown,
But only yellow to Viera was shown.
The Wednesday crowd went completely mad,
But what happened next was really bad.

The Hillsborough crowd went into a hush,
When Di Canio gave the ref a push.
As Paul Alcock hit the ground,
You could hardly hear a sound.

Later that night on Match of the Day,
Danny Wilson agreed it wasn't fair play.
Now Di Canio will have to wait,
Until the FA decide his fate.

Matt Angus (12)
Newbold Community School

EVERYONE'S GONE CRAZY

My brother said the sea waves
So yesterday I waved to the sea,
But it didn't wave back.

My dad told me bottles have necks
So I asked my dad where's its head?

My mum told me chairs have legs
So I looked at the one in the kitchen
And found it had no feet.

My sister said that needles have eyes
But all I could see was a hole.

My grandad said the door was ajar
But I couldn't put anything in it.

My teacher said I should pull my socks up
But I was wearing tights.

My uncle said there was a chip in the computer
But I couldn't eat it.

I don't know what's got into everyone,
I told them they were crazy
But they didn't answer me, they just laughed.

Sarah Farris (13)
Newbold Community School

HOMEWORK

'Homework is boring!' I say to my mum
It's full of writing, and drawing and loads of old sums.
I think we do enough learning at school
Who thought up all these silly rules?
It's the only thing me and my brother agree on.
That homework is boring, something to be sick on!
Writing and drawing and more of those sums,
Why can't we just go home to have fun?

Jacqueline Smith (12)
Newbold Community School

Y2K

The year 2000
What a time
Y2K will not be forgotten
Well . . . not in my mind.

Millennium Dome
London Eye
Dome disaster
The Eye can spy.

Millennium bug
A non event
Millions of pounds
Needlessly spent.

Olympic Games
Firework display
British gold
Hip, hip, hooray!

Katie Simpson (12)
Newbold Community School

TED THE TROUT

There once was a trout called Ted
He had a peculiar head
He loved to go to bed
His motorpike was red
He went to get wed
His wife loved to eat bread
She ate a piece of lead
Got poisoned and ended up dead
'Oh dear,' he said 'I've just got wed'
Along came fisherman Ned
He filled his hook with bread
Ted ate the bread
Was whipped out of the water and hit on the head
Ted was dead and became supper for Ned.

Mark Gascoyne (12)
Newbold Community School

THERE ONCE WAS A . . .

There once was a teacher called Cox
Who smelt of old, woollen socks,
When the children went near her
They used to compare her to a sly, old fox.

There once was a woman called Jan
Who loved to eat raspberry jam
She was rather into fine ham.

There once was a man called Peter
Who had a terrible urge for pizza
He ate it with garlic
And then smelt of Horlicks.

Emma Lankford (12)
Newbold Community School

THE RACE

The starter's flag,
The surge of muscular bodies.
Hooves flashing in the autumn sun,
Crouched bodies of the jockeys.
Silks that are up in front, red and green,
Horses coats with a healthy sheen.
Strides coming faster and longer.
Trying to find the best route,
On the lush, green grass,
Mud splattering on hard hats.
The roar of the crowds on the stands,
Jockeys urging their horses forwards,
With crop or hand,
Urging, urging.
Straining necks and bodies,
Every ounce of heart and courage.
One length, two lengths,
The chestnut thoroughbred,
Carrying green and red,
Surges in front,
To the roar of the crowd,
She sweeps under the wire.
Proud in the winner's circle,
Heaving flanks,
Head held high,
Ears pricked and alert.
Proudly she stands,
All 17 hands.

Sally Davies (12)
Newbold Community School

MY OWL POEM

The owl flies silently at night
He hunts his prey while in flight.
He feeds upon mice or sometimes on rats
But for him a real feast is a couple of bats.
He lives up in trees or sometimes in towers
Where he sleeps away all the daylight hours.
His cry is so mournful he says 'Tu-Whit Tu-Whoo'
Which probably means I'm looking at you.
For his eyes are so big and so very round
He can stare for hours without making a sound.

Ben Watkinson (13)
Newbold Community School

ME AND MY FAMILY

My mum is a nurse
My dad is a dentist
My sister likes dancing
My little brother is teething.
My other little brother is crying
My nan likes doing bingo
My grandma likes riding big rides
My aunty is a model.
My uncle is a policeman
My other uncle is a pilot
My other aunty is a great actress
My other uncle is on the booze.
My other aunty is a housewife
My cousins are singers
And me, of course, likes acting
And that is all!

Chantelle Oldfield (12)
Newbold Community School

DOLPHINS

Swimming in the sea,
Jumping in the air,
What a pretty sight,
Swimming day and night.

Dolphins doing tricks,
Making people laugh,
Watch the dolphins dive,
Watch the dolphins glide.

The dolphin show has just begun,
So come along and join the fun,
Bring your family and your friends,
The dolphin show will never end.

The dolphins will show you a good time,
You'll watch their act,
You'll watch them chime,
But right now sit back and enjoy the show.

Kelli Cocking (12)
Newbold Community School

DERBYSHIRE

The black alarm clock sitting on the bedside table
Waiting to go off beep beep
Crash against the wall as we throw it
Springs go flying everywhere
Time tastes like a sizzling strip of bacon
For lunch a plate of nice chips
For tea a nice Sunday dinner
Time smells like Mum's cooking.

Paul Murphy (11)
Newbold Community School

DEAD PETS!

Once I had a cat called Toffee,
Who drank a lot of coffee,
He stayed up all night,
Even when it was light,
He gave the dog a scare,
When he glared that terrible glare,
After a while,
He was as hard as a tile.
He was dead,
Well that's what everyone said.

Once I had a gerbil called Chips,
Who liked to bite upper lips.
He chomped his way through all my family,
Even my best friend Emily.
So in the end
Everyone went round the bend,
They picked him up,
Tossed him in a cup
And threw him in the river.

Once I had a lot of pets,
They were always going to the vets.
All the pets I had,
Seemed to be so mad.
They all died
Or got fried.
From now on,
Pets are gone,
I've left that all behind.
Instead I've started fishing,
So I can kill them all I'm wishing.

Philippa Brown (12)
Newbold Community School

BIKES, I LOVE THEM

Bikes, I love 'em
I cannot leave them alone
I like to play
Jumping bikes
I love 'em
They come big
Small, medium
They come in
Different styles
BMX trick
Stunt normal
And I cannot tell you all the styles
Giant, Trek, Raleigh
And so many more bikes
I love 'em, big ones, small and middle size ones.
I just cannot leave them alone
They're brill and cool
But I feel sorry for them
Because they *go*
Through so much
Hammer . . .

Robert Ward (11)
Newbold Community School

SPLAT

I was waiting patiently near my web
Ready to land on a pupil's head
I get ready to pounce in mid air
But I start to swing like I'm at the fair
I plummet to the ground
But don't make a sound
I saw a boy who was rather fat
Then next I was splat.

I was flying along
Singing my song
Feeling rather hungry
I saw a worm
I swooped down into the path of an oncoming
4X4
The driver didn't look
Until I was stuck
In front of where he was sat
So that was that *Splat!*

Stephen Barnett (12)
Newbold Community School

MY LITTLE BROTHER

I don't like my little brother,
He's always getting me in trouble,
He's always going,
'Mum, Mum, tell him to stop it.'
Always stealing my things,
Always changing the channel,
Always being silly,
Always blaming things on me,
Always calling me names,
Always disturbing me,
Always playing on my games,
Always hiding my school books,
Always taking my money,
Always taking my pens and pencils,
Always waking me up in a morning,
Always, always, getting on my nerves,
So please someone get rid of him -
I'll pay you!

Tom Fisher (12)
Newbold Community School

THE BEACH

Waves beating on the chalky cliffs,
Sun beaming down on the golden sand,
Clear, blue sea shimmering,
Dolphins leaping out the clear water.
Shipwrecks washed up on the shore,
People tanning in the sun,
Waves, white and foamy,
Sand, golden and gritty,
Sand, seeping through your feet,
Shells scattered on the sore,
Crabs, hiding in rock pools,
Seagulls soaring in the sky,
Sea caves in the cliffs,
Flags on sandcastles blowing in the breeze,
Seaweed swirling in the shallow water.

Rachel Barratt (12)
Newbold Community School

TORTOISE!

Plodding slowly down the garden path,
Never daring to go near the bird bath,
Slow plod, slow plod! In the dry leaves,
Then he reaches the long grass then he has to weave -
Round the plant pot, through the mud, up the spade and into bed
It sleeps in a bundle of leaves and hay
And for a long time that's where it will stay
When it finally awakes it plods back to the garden pile of leaves,
Then goes to investigate the garden path,
Making sure not to go near the bird bath,
Looking for food!

Rebecca Yeowart (13)
Newbold Community School

THE SUPERMARKET MANAGER

He was very jolly
And liked to save people's lolly
So people could put cheap food in their shopping trolleys
Biscuits and honey
Save lots of money
Crisps and sweets
Were very cheap treats.
Tinned food and fresh
Whatever you could see
He started to give the food away for free.
People came one after another
The fruit, the veg, cereal and pop
Everything went out of the shop
Even to the last pork chop.

Laura Blissett (12)
Newbold Community School

THE MOON

The moon is a universal object,
that rotates around the world,
lighting up the darkness with a single
moonbeam's light.
The sun gives the moon the power,
to shine upon the earth.
Without the moon they'd be no light,
shining in the sky at night.
You can see it through your window,
a gigantic silver ball,
it looks so near but is so far,
a planet surrounded by stars.

Elizabeth Huggins (11)
Newbold Community School

DOLPHINS

Dolphins swimming in the deep blue sea,
Tossing and turning as happy as can be.
There, they are somersaulting in the air,
They never get nasty they even play fair.
My favourite things are dolphins
And I go mad when they're put in tuna tins.
So listen to me and take my advice,
Dolphins are so very nice.
When I was on holiday I stroked one called Chubber
And when you touch them they feel like rubber.

Kourtney Yates (12)
Newbold Community School

HOME SWEET HOME

Home sweet home,
The big warm chairs,
And the long winding stairs,
With the cosy, warm rooms,
And the hidden, black brooms,
The burning wood fire,
And the suits on hire,
The tall hat stands
And the noise of the brass band,
The big fur hats
And the outdoor mats,
The lovely food smells
And the big, shiny shells
The lovely, tasty food
And the happy family mood.
Home sweet home.

Laura Grimwade (12)
Newbold Community School

THE BEAST

Lurking, working in a cave making metal claws,
Under a hill,
Where he will kill,
There will be blood on the floors.
He burnt his skin
And smells of paraffin,
He has evil eyes
And all around him are flies.
He wears one big, black welly,
Beware, he is very smelly.
Think of him if you dare,
He is your worst nightmare.
He will get you while asleep,
Stay awake, counting sheep.

Ryan Kemp (11)
Newbold Community School

WET WEATHER

Wet weather makes me feel glum
The weatherman said it would be sunny today, he's so dumb
Wet weather is boring, there's nothing to do
I hope it stops today so I can go hang out with my crew
Wet weather!
Rain bouncing off the ground
All around me everywhere I look
Rain, rain sloshing down the drain
All these puddles everywhere
I wish I could sneak out, I wouldn't dare
It seems like it is here to stay
Rain, rain go away, come back another day.

Matthew Taylor (12)
Newbold Community School

DOLPHIN

Swimming through the sea,
Acting playfully.
Somersaulting in the air,
Swimming around everywhere.
Over and under the deep blue sea,
Catching fishes for their tea.
Exploring distant shores,
Their brains the size of yours.
They love all mankind,
But don't like to be confined.
Wonderful, magical and free,
Their kingdom is the sea.
Intelligent and beautiful,
Dolphins are my favourite animal.

Angharad Stanley (12)
Newbold Community School

THE SPIDER

The colours of the web, they shine
Very neat, precise and fine
In his web the spider spins
The fly's been caught, the spider wins
In the tangled web that has been spun
The cobweb glistens in the sun
Hanging on, the web is secure
Onto the branch, not near the floor
The spider is on the move again
Looking for prey, unsure when
He will find another fly
Caught in his web about to die.

Anya Taylor (12)
Newbold Community School

WINTER POEM

Cold and freezing winter
It's not as bad as when you've got a splinter
Ice skating on the lake
Then we can eat Christmas cake
A Christmas feed
Is what we need
Lots of Christmas songs
So we can't go wrong
I think you know
Fluffy, white, cold snow
A Christmas feed
Is what we need
On top of the tree is a star
The biggest present would be a car
A mobile phone would do
And I'm sure you want one too
A Christmas feed
Is what we need
It's terrible when you walk to school
When snow is in a yucky pool
You can have snowball fights
As long as the lamp posts are alight
A Christmas feed
Is what we need.

Emma Mellor (11)
Newbold Community School

SPIDER

I like spiders
I like them when they run
The spiders are fat
He is hairy
His eyes are big
His legs are like rubber
His body is chunky
Spiders are fast
Spiders are black
I like spiders, I would like a spider
Spiders are sometimes slow
Spiders are good web spinners
He is hairy
His legs are rubber and thin
Spiders have got eight legs
Spiders are fun.

Lauren Tailby (11)
Newbold Community School

THE MOON

The moon is like milk, creamy-white
The moon is like a skull, spooky
A face always there watching us
The moon is like a white chocolate button

The moon is like a pizza
Round bits on it
The moon is like a cave
Dark, cold, full of mystery
The moon.

Sam Walker (12)
Newbold Community School

MY GUINEA PIG

My guinea pigs Candy and Kirsty,
Are nearly four years old.
One is just plain brown
And the other has ginger on her back.
They live in a hutch,
My dad made it you know.

Now they're in the shed,
But that's only in the winter.
They live outside with a run attached,
That's only in the summer though.
But in spring and autumn,
It's in the shed or outside.

But since we go on holiday soon,
I will not be seeing them.
But they will be fine (I hope)!
So when I get back they will be with me again,
So I'm going to say 'Bye girlies!'

Hannah Scott (11)
Newbold Community School

THE RIVER

The river is cold, fast and long,
Twisty, curly, a watery song.
It gushes across the crisp, dry rocks,
Water spraying at my bone-dry socks.
The birds are singing, the trees are blowing,
But nothing stops the river flowing.
The river is cold, fast and long,
Twisty, curly, a watery song.

Luke Preston (11)
Newbold Community School

BOOK!

Some books are boring and some books are good,
Some books are really expensive, some are not.
Some books are picture books and some books are 100 pages long,
Some are only 30 and some are only 10!
Some have no pictures, just a great mass of writing
And some are a bit of both.
Some books are all I want to read and some books I really don't,
My school reader is good, it's called Whispers in the Graveyard.
My other reader wasn't that good, I really didn't enjoy it,
I think it went on forever!
My friends got really interesting books which made me very mad,
Because I wanted a book that was sad.
Before I didn't like to read but now it's all I want to do!
Books are the biz, you ought to try reading too!
Books, books, books, books are great,
Books, books, books, books, books.

Kelly Cotterill (11)
Newbold Community School

WHEN I WAS AT PRIMARY SCHOOL

When I was at Primary School,
I always remember our swimming pool.
When I got in the football team,
My kit was very bright and green.

When I was at Primary School,
Me and my mates were really cool.
My favourite lesson was PE,
But Miss always forgot the key.

When I was at Primary School,
We had to sit on a little stool.
School dinners were very nice,
And for dessert I always had chocolate mice.

When I was at Primary School,
I liked to play with my hammering tool.
The only thing I didn't like,
Was when Miss gave us a really big fright.

Daniel Barker (12)
Newbold Community School

MY DOG

I'm the only one that likes my dog
If you know what I mean
He's done everything he could
Even sent the next door's baby green
He's peed on the sofa, ripped the postman's pants
He's vandalised the street and made the misses prance
I'm the only one that likes my dog
If you know what I mean
He's done everything he could
Even made my sister scream
He unholyed the holy water, buried my mum's necklace
He tore apart the gate and threw it in the stream
I'm the only one that likes my dog
If you know what I mean
He's the worst mongrel you've ever seen
But he's all right I suppose.

Jack Needham (11)
Newbold Community School

TV

TV I hate thee
TV look out for me

TV show me the way
TV I have one thing to say

TV you make me jolly and gay
TV I will make you pay

TV you hate me today
TV why news all day

TV hip hip hooray
TV you're okay today

TV all day and night
TV good stuff for my delight.

Dannie Methven (11)
Newbold Community School

FRIENDS

Friends are like pens
If they don't work
You throw them away.
Friends are like string
If you can't wrap it
Around your little finger
It's no use!
Friends are like knives
They can hurt you deeply
But friends are like fags
Once you've had one
You want another!

Robert Garner (12)
Newbold Community School

ME

My name is Emma,
I am an alcoholic,
My hobbies are swimming and riding my bike,
My best friends from primary school are Lindsey, Michelle and Sarah.
My friends at Newbold are Lauren, Emma and Gemma.
I have brown eyes,
I have brown hair,
That makes me a brunette.
I'm very small compared to my friends,
I have a hamster called Speedy,
I have two brothers, one sister, one sister-in-law and one nephew.
My favourite book is one of the Goosebumps books.
We also have a fish at home
And my form tutor is Mrs Waller.

Emma Swale (11)
Newbold Community School

FAIRY NUFF

I am a little fairy
I've come to fetch your tooth
But now I think it's really time
That you were told the truth

For years you've thought that it was me
That always came around
And crept into your room at night
And didn't make a sound

The next day came and you got up
And shouted 'I've got money'
You really thought that I had been
But no it was your mummy!

Jodie Fareham (12)
Newbold Community School

CHEETAH

I've got spots,
I run very fast.
I'll challenge a hare,
And I won't come last.

I look like a leopard,
But I've got more spots.
They might not want much food,
But I want lots.

I've got spotty ears,
I've got long legs.
I hate clothes
And thank goodness I don't hang on
A line with pegs.

I don't listen to music
Or watch telly.
I could race a car,
On a rally.

Gemma Sellars (11)
Newbold Community School

CATS

Cats, cats, black as the night
Eyes dazzle clear and bright
When the stars glisten the cats will glare
With a sleek, sly stare
Sleep all day keeping away from the light
Cats are black, black as the night.

Rebecca Platts (12)
Newbold Community School

PENTEWAN CRABS

Its beady black eyes
And pincers that tear
All the little kids shout out 'Beware!'
Do not climb the toilet seat
Because Pentewan crabs can jump six feet.

Just like chicken and good to eat
But when you're on the toilet watch out for your feet
So do not climb the toilet seat
Because Pentewan crabs can jump six feet.

Their ugly black body
And legs that are long
With a huge hollow mouth about ten metres long
So do not climb the toilet seat
Because Pentewan crabs can jump six feet

Its body is rough, hard and strong
Like the one of a tortoise that is weird and long
So do not climb the toilet seat
Because Pentewan crabs can jump six feet.

They aren't so big but frightening to eyes
For they don't know how to make a disguise
They hide under weed and make the image or a rock
But if you go near them they'll come out in a flock
So do not climb the toilet seat
Because Pentewan crabs can jump six feet.

Franco Hardy (11)
Newbold Community School

ANIMALS

Dogs are as fast as a cat
Cats are as thin as a rat
Rats are as loud as a dragon
Dragons are as fast as flies
Flies are as small as a bird
Birds are as pretty as a monkey
Monkeys are as cheeky as a frog
Frogs are as slimy as a fish
Fish are as ugly as a spider
Spiders are as fierce as a bear
Bears are as hungry as a lion
Lions are as lazy as a slug
Slugs are as slow as an elephant
Elephants are as naughty as a dog.

James Watkinson (11)
Newbold Community School

THE POEM

The teachers at our school
Are the ones we aim to please,
In English we must write a poem
I'll skip through it with ease.

I'll write a poem 'bout birds that sing,
I'll do one about a skyscraper.
I'll tell a tale of a ten-foot whale,
Or shall I just write about paper?

I will write about girls and boys,
No! I'll speak of a pool.
On second thoughts, a monster is better,
Wait, I'll write about *school!*

The poems done, it's all over,
I only wrote a bit.
Now, for the poem that I wrote,
Low and behold, *this is it!'*

Aden Carlile (12)
Newbold Community School

MY LITTLE SISTER

My little sister is a pain
She drives me insane
She is always begging me to play football
And it drives me up the wall
She always used to cry at night
Now we always fight
At night I love to escape
To enjoy my own space
But as soon as I get in
She starts all over again
I can't wait till I leave home
Because then I can be alone
Every morning she never wants to go to school
Then my dad is always shouting
And they finally give in.

Michelle Prince (12)
Newbold Community School

THE CAT

My bright green eyes glint through the dark,
As I sneak around the park,
As my tail whips round the bend,
My trusty claws I will not lend,
The blaring headlights of a car,
First it's near and then it's far,
I quickly dodge out of the way,
And carry on along my way,
Past the slide and past the swings,
And past all sorts of man-made things,
And then at last I find my prey,
It will not live another day,
And then I carry this little mouse,
Back to my lovely warm house.

Lindsey Starkey (11)
Newbold Community School

ANIMALS AND PETS

Elephants are tall,
Ants are very small,
Spiders run,
Whilst caterpillars crawl.

Hamsters are funny,
Others like it when it's sunny,
Worms are slimy,
But monkeys and gorillas are hairy.

Wild rats are disgusting,
Mice like things that are rustling,
Birds fly in the sky,
Ladybirds climb on leaves and trees.

Bees like honey,
Foxes are very cunning,
Scorpions live in the desert,
Lions live in the zoo.

Emma Greenwood (11)
Newbold Community School

STORM

There's a storm outside
It's knocking on my door
I'm curled up small
Lying in my bed
The storm's getting nearer
It's getting louder to my hearing
I think it's coming up the stairs
Creeping closer all the time
My windows are rattling
My lights are flickering
Bang! Bang! Bang! On my bedroom door
Suddenly my door flies open
It's creeping towards my bed
'Dad you scared me half to death!'

Stephanie Krence (13)
Newbold Community School

LIFE, LOVE AND LAUGHS

Life, love and laughs,
What a wonderful world we have,
People dancing and having fun.
Ball gowns and wine,
That's the way I love to dine.
Life, love and laughs,
My past will always last.
The way I used to read my comics
And when I played in the sand pit at school
I will never forget it.
Life, love and laughs,
That's how I like to live,
In happiness and love,
Yes, in happiness and love.

Laura Jennison (12)
Newbold Community School

FLYING THINGS

The aeroplane!
Flying in the sky
High above the fluffy clouds
On a winter's day.

The helicopter!
Propelling so fast
Taking passengers
To and from places.

Birds!
Soaring through the sky
Flipping and folding his wings
Ever so madly.

Rebecca Page (12)
Newbold Community School

ANIMAL POEMS!

Long trunk
Big ears
Ivory tusks
Rough skin
Watery eyes
Clammy feet
Stubby nails
Wisps of hair
My elephant friend.

Long legs
Beady eyes
Stabbing claws
Burnt orange shell
Sand covered back
Fat, curvy body
Pointy toes
Rock hard shell
My sealife creature, the crab.

Long ears
Twitching nose
Silky fur
Beaming eyes
Slender feet
Spiky nails
Drooping whiskers
Bobbing tail
My pet bunny.

Amy Read (12)
Newbold Community School

MEMORIES

The lone figure standing by the plunging, sapphire waves,
The wise moon suspended in the immense blanket
of the star-studded sky,
The single eagle soaring high above the earth's unspoilt surface,
The lonely shell lying on the golden beach, untouched by human hands,
The forlorn child wandering, lonely, friendless,
The solitary statue frozen in the midst of time.
The memories of a lifetime entwining with my dreams,
The glittering shoal of fish that swim below the glistening waves,
The millions of tiny stars that shine through the winter's darkness,
The flock of geese that glide through the endless skies,
The cluster of tiny turtles, each one scanning the silver beaches,
The gang of children, guiltless as to what they had just done,
My memories are my thoughts and dreams -
But my dreams entwine with my memories.

Phoebe Woods (12)
Newbold Community School

MY MAGIC BOX

I will capture in my box
a wicked miaow of a witch's black cat
a fish swimming in the clear blue sea
the roar of a gigantic lion.

I will trap in the box
a swirl of a hurricane
and a drop of the Atlantic Ocean
the smell of the Mediterranean Sea
as I float gently over the waves.

I will drop in the box
a seagull swooping down for brightly coloured fish
a shimmering diamond from the dark old caverns
the tenth planet or a second Christmas every year.

My box is created from oceans of dark blue silk
and crafted from stars and distant planets
the lock is made from shells from zooming fish
the key is made from a great white shark's tooth.

Karen Dove (11)
Newbold Community School

PICTURE PORTRAIT

I've got a picture of a painting of a person posing for a portrait
Posing for her portrait in an old-fashioned purple dress
An old-fashioned purple dress with a lilac printed pattern
Lilac printed pattern printed perfectly leading to the neck
The neck hole surrounded by a decorative lacy pink frill
Lacy pink frill wrapped around a pink podgy neck
Pink podgy neck supporting a perfectly posed head
A perfectly posed head presenting a pink plump face
A pink plump face with two dark piercing piggy-eyes
Piercing piggy-eyes to match a pretty piggy-nose
A pretty piggy-nose set between two neatly powdered cheeks
Powdered cheeks placed above a pimpleless chin
A pimpleless chin placed below a perfectly posed set of plump pink lips
This picture is of a portrait
A portrait of a person
The person in this picture displayed for all eyes to see
The person in this picture is as pretty as can be
The person in this picture couldn't be anyone else but me!

Debbie Davies (12)
Newbold Community School

BOOKS!

Books are very useful
They open and they close
You chase them from the library
And hold them to your nose.

Books for little babies
Some that make a noise
Some with soft and squeezy bits
The favourite of toys.

Books with big bright pictures
Lots to make you giggle
Some with funny, silly bits
With pop-ups in the middle.

Books to read for hours
Open up the story
Find yourself quite petrified
Wicked and so gory.

Books, paperbacks and hardbacks
Something for all ages
Transported to another world
As you gobble up the pages.

Lucy Chambers (12)
Newbold Community School

TEACHERS

Teachers sometimes drive me up the wall
They're oh so big and oh so tall
They think we're meant to worship them
'Get on with your work, here's a pen.'

'Right up to the headmaster you stupid boy.
I'm sick of you playing with that stupid toy!'
It comes to the end of the day, at last!
That teacher's livin' way back in the past.

They don't let you have any fun
In PE they just make you run and run
In history they just dig up the past
To tell you to start writing and fast

I love drama
It makes me feel a lot calmer
The teachers are a lot nicer
They just take you for who you are
And they don't take cases way too far.

That's another day over
I'm off on holiday to Dover
Bye-bye teachers, I'll not miss you
See ya school - whoo hoo.

Kathryn Shedden (12)
Newbold Community School

WHY I AM A PUNK

When I'm a punk I get drunk and have a dump,
then go to bed with my ted.
I had a fright in the middle of the night,
then looked back and saw my bike.
I went on it bumping down the stairs,
then a hare ran in the door.
I squashed its head and all the brains flew out,
I went for a ride and then died, came back to life
and saw I was banging on my gran's door.
She called me a nutter then I muttered
'You're an old ducker.'
She came out with a pan smacking my tum,
I called her a big old witch
and then she turned me into a big fat twig.
That's the life of a punk.

Jonathan Dean Carver (13)
Newbold Community School

ALL I COULD DO WAS SCREAM HELP!

One day I was running down the pitch
And I got a great itch
And I fell down a great ditch
Come on someone help me!

Please help, please
I think I have a broken ankle
I need help
Come on help me!

Some stupid kids came to see
But all they did was laugh at me
I think they came to see the bloody mess
I couldn't say my name, I was in shock.

So I screamed and screamed
And a teacher came and said
'Get out you stupid boy
You're making an awful racket.'
So he lifted me out with a broken ankle.

Dean Mitchell (12)
Newbold Community School

My School Day

My mum shouts yet again,
She can't half be a pain.
'I'm having five more minutes Mum.'
'Don't be so dumb!'
As I crawl from my bed
In comes my Uncle Ted.
'Are you ready for school yet Jay?'
'No Ted, I'm walking today.'
I rush down the stairs, 'Bye Mum, bye Claire.'
I get to school with two minutes to spare.
English is first followed by maths, PE and art.
I had a great day at school (not),
But a nice walk home with my mate Bart.
When I got home my sister's already there.
'I'm back before you.'
'I don't care!'
'Oh yes, I nearly forgot, I've got you an alarm clock.'
That means no more sore throats for my mum.

Richard Pyatt (12)
Newbold Community School

SHARKS ARE COOL

Sharks
Have
A really
Really good sight
Sharks also have a really nasty bite
So stay out of the water in the day or the night
Are you afraid of the shark?
Everyone else
Maybe
Sharks like all things for their tea
Could
You swim with a shark
Could I?
I'll let you know I can't!

Kristopher Kemp (13)
Newbold Community School

SPACE IS . . .

Space is dark
Space is cold
Space is very, very old

Space is large
Space is starry
Space is very far away

Space is mysterious
Space is cloudy
Space is weird and unknown
No hi-tech mobile phones

Space is a place not for the human race
It is unreal
It is wild
It is an eternity.

Kylie Bonsell (12)
Newbold Community School

THE FIFTH OF NOVEMBER

Remember, remember the fifth of November
It comes once a year.

Remember, remember the fifth of November
Fun, fireworks and good cheer.

Remember, remember the fifth of November
A time for Guy Fawkes to fear.

Remember, remember the fifth of November
Only Guy Fawkes must burn and sear.

Remember, remember the fifth of November
From the bonfire keep clear.

Remember, remember the fifth of November
It only comes once a year.

Rachel Hall (12)
Newbold Community School

HAMSTER

I have a pet,
he is fluffy and white,
he sleeps all day,
and comes out at night.
He runs in a wheel
and makes a racket,
I brought him last year
and he cost a packet.
I called him Pebbles,
I think he knows his name.
He lets me stroke him,
he's ever so tame.
He's a rodent of course,
do you know what kind?
If he's loose in the house
he's hard to find.

Faye Portas (13)
Newbold Community School

THE GARDEN ROSE

The garden rose lonely and old
like a light bulb always bright
A flame, a star as it twinkles
in the morning frost.

Darren Parkin (11)
Newbold Community School

SWEETS

Sweets are good
They taste real nice,
But take my advice,
Your teeth may rot,
For too many sweets,
You'll have a job,
With not a lot.
But we all love sweets
So we'll never listen,
Even if our teeth are missing.
Chew and crunch them,
Suck them as well,
Eat too many
And feel unwell.
But sweets do taste very nice,
So just ignore my advice.

Daniel Plumb (12)
Newbold Community School

THE MAN FROM CHESTER

There was an old man from Chester
Where seven small children did pester
They threw some large stones
Which broke most of his bones
And displeased the old man from Chester.

Matthew Foster (12)
Newbold Community School

HATE

I hate you, I hate you
You're always there
The grease in my hair
The hole in my sock
The poo on my shoe
The mould on the wall
The wax in my ear
The muck on my book
The burn in my carpet
The broken down lift
The shattered window
The gone-off perfume
The snapped ruler
The mouldy tomato
The flaky paintwork
The rusty pipe
Oh I hate you, I hate you
You're always there.

Natalie Bramley (12)
Newbold Community School

SCHOOL

School, school, school,
If you follow the rules,
It can be cool.

We like school,
Because we follow rules,
And it can be cool.

You have to use a bag
And your mum has to nag
For you to get all your books in your bag
The night before school
My bag is new
The colour is cool blue
I've got pencil cases like cats
And rubbers like Winnie the Pooh.

Katie Louise Bowen (11)
Newbold Community School

AUTUMN

Autumn is my favourite time
Sometimes wet
Sometimes fine
The leaves go brown, the flowers die
And big black clouds fill the sky.

We find conkers on the ground
The open shells are all around
Playing out in coats and hats
No more use for cricket bats.

The nights draw in
The wind turns cold
Hallowe'en's here
With monsters bold.

Paul Cartledge (11)
Newbold Community School

MY BROTHER

Dexter my brother
Plays on his computer
Dexter my brother
Plays with his Scalextric
Dexter my brother
Plays with Lego
Dexter my brother
Plays with me.

Gregg Vickery (13)
Parkwood School

SLEEP

When I go to sleep
I close my eyes, I don't peep
I don't have to count sheep
Who are trying to leap
My eyes shut I keep
When I go to sleep.

Terry Critchlow (14)
Parkwood School

MY DOG

I love my dog
She is called Pip
She likes to play with me
I love my dog
She likes to kip
When she's had a walk with me.

Jane Winson (15)
Parkwood School

MY HOLIDAY

A caravan is where I stay
On the sand I like to play
For an ice-cream I have to pay
When I'm away on holiday.

Robert Magee (13)
Parkwood School

MY DOG

My dog is such a gentle soul,
She sleeps all the time,
But when the post lady comes to the door,
She drags her across the floor.

Victoria Pratt (11)
St Mary's RC High School, Chesterfield

RAINDROPS

Plip, plip, plop,
Plip, plip, plop.
Look at that big raindrop,
Oh no! It went down the drain,
Oh well, it was only rain.

Lara Shepherd (12)
St Mary's RC High School, Chesterfield

BASKING SHARKS

B asking sharks and bull sharks,
A wesome and huge, swimming in the dark,
S harks, sharks, sharks, they frighten me,
K ings, kings, kings of the sea.
I n the day, at night they're there,
N imbly swimming without a care,
G roups of sharks swimming free, and steadily.

S harks, sharks, sharks, ferocious fish of the sea,
H uge, huge, huge, they frighten me,
A round and around they do swim,
R eally big but very nimble,
K illers of the sea.

Lauren Miller (13)
St Mary's RC High School, Chesterfield

MUSICAL WORLD

Music can be joyful
Music can be sad
Music can be tearful
Music can be mad.

There is funky pop
And dreary classic
There's head banging rock
And R 'n' B magic.

The musical world
Brings people together
It can make you feel good
And as light as a feather.

Amie Ward (12)
St Mary's RC High School, Chesterfield

FASHION!

Fashion!
In one minute, out the next,
Gotta get those shoes, gotta get that dress.
Stripes, spots, squares, dots,
High shoes, busters lots.
Buy the clothes by the load,
Season's over - new wardrobe.

Carrie Wilson (13)
St Mary's RC High School, Chesterfield

AUTUMN

A   ll the leaves are falling,
U   nder my shoes they are
T   urning crisp and brown,
U   nder my feet they sound,
M   aking a crunching
N   oise.

Michael Foster (14)
St Mary's RC High School, Chesterfield

SAUSAGE DOGS

Sausage dogs are big and round,
Their belly trails along the ground,
They eat all the sausages that they see
And they eat sausages for every tea.

Patrick Grant (13)
St Mary's RC High School, Chesterfield

BONFIRE NIGHT

It's dark outside the only light coming
From the bonfire, red and orange and yellow.
The fireworks light up the sky,
The crackling from the fireworks and
Spitting from the fire.
The crowds are cheering as the
Catherine wheel goes round, pink and blue and red.

The morning after there's a smell of
Smoke, you can see remains of the
Fireworks smoke still rising from the fire.

Orange - is the sunset on a dream holiday,
Yellow - is the colour of the sunflowers in summer,
Red - is the devil on Hallowe'en,
Black - is the midnight sky.

Clare Frankish (14)
St Mary's RC High School, Chesterfield

YELLOW

Yellow like sunshine spilling through my window
On a warm summer's morning,
Yellow like a field of daffodils in the
Middle of spring,
Yellow like butter melting on warm toast,
Yellow like stars in the dark midnight sky,
Yellow like soft sand on a warm beach,
Yellow like the feeling I have inside of me,
When someone makes me feel special.

Louise Harbottle (14)
St Mary's RC High School, Chesterfield

WHAT IF EVERYTHING WAS EDIBLE

Imagine if we were made of chocolate gateau,
Whipped cream for our hair,
Smarties as eyes,
We wouldn't have to care,
Because if we were eaten,
We'd immediately grow back,
Nothing would ever melt,
But sun, we would not lack.
The great ball of fire would actually be ice-cream.
It would rain chocolate drops
And the best thing would be,
We'd be able to eat lots
And we'd never get fat!

Lucy Ashton (12)
St Mary's RC High School, Chesterfield

LONELINESS!

I sit up in my room
All alone
Thinking who could I have been
I could have been a superstar
But no I'm just alone
On my own,
I will probably die alone
It's the worse thing in the world
Don't ever suffer
Loneliness.

Rachel Edwards
St Mary's RC High School, Chesterfield

WHO AM I?

In this world everything is big to me,
To the tallest giant, to the littlest strand of grass,
There's lots of me, who all look like me, but
They are just different sizes on the other side of the Universe.
I work hard every day and night, working hard
Making sure everything is right.
Gathering harvest in the autumn, to prepare
For the horrible chilling winter, so we don't
Starve to death and feel like splinters.
I am a worker, working for the queen,
Helping to build her palace and keeping ours clean.
We travel in very big groups,
Day by day, collecting leaves, bits and bobs,
On our way, to keep us warm, till the sunny day.
We are pests in people's homes,
But we get trampled on and no one even knows.
Our countries are big and in lines,
We don't hurt the evil giants, who trample on us to death,
But the giants aren't as evil as the hairy
Hoover who eats us for tea.
So be considerate to us, as we do no harm to you,
We may give you the creeps,
But you give us them too.

What am I?

Maria Lazari (14)
St Mary's RC High School, Chesterfield

SHARKY, SHARKY . . . SHARK

Here Sharky Shark
Come with us through the dark.
To scare and have a lark,
With me and the other sharks.

Sharky Sharks straight as a dart,
In through the dark,
Into the light for a quick bite,
'Ahhhhh!'

Russell Stubbings (12)
St Mary's RC High School, Chesterfield

CHRISTMAS POEM

The advent calendars are in the shop,
We're Christmas shopping, no time to stop.
Sledging in the snow having fun all day,
Small children all waiting for Santa's sleigh.
Carol singers out in the street,
Hot mince pies scrumptious to eat.
Friends and family on our Christmas card list,
We hope, oh we hope, that there's no one we've missed.
Christmas tree - what type? What size?
Tinsel and baubles to dazzle our eyes.
Bright colourful lights in windows and trees,
Wrapping up presents, we're hoping will please.
The three wise men who followed the star,
Are put in the crib - how near we are!
Rudolph and the reindeer prepare to pull the sleigh,
Hang up your stocking, it's only hours away,
The turkey is ready and the family arrive,
Dancing blue flames bring the pud alive.
Presents have been opened, there's just crackers to pull,
Everyone's tummy is full, full, full.
Remember . . .
Good will to all men and peace on Earth,
We have Christmas to celebrate Jesus' birth.

Patrick Boyle (14)
St Mary's RC High School, Chesterfield

GENERATION SEA

The sea is beautiful,
With all its creatures
And every little bit
Has its different features.

With all its coral
And fish galore,
Is the reason why
We should look after it more.

The sea should be blue,
But in some places it's grey,
With all the rubbish in it,
Who's surprised anyway?

So we need to keep it clean,
For generations to come,
That means all of it,
Not just some.

Rachel Edworthy (12)
St Mary's RC High School, Chesterfield

WINTER

As snowflakes carpeted the ground from
Beneath the blistering cold and frost that we seek.
We all love winter so that's what we wonder,
Until we get hail which shoots down like thunder.
Never we believe how strong weather can be,
But when it destroys and terrorises
We can only watch and see.

Jonathan Fields (11)
St Mary's RC High School, Chesterfield

BETTER

'The cancer's gone' the doctor said,
My feet fell down like lumps of lead.
'You mean, it's worked, you think I'm cured,
Sitting here I've been so bored.
Do you know the plans I've been making,
Every night I kept on waking,
Feeling this thing growing inside,
Making me want to run and hide.'

Rebecca Cartledge (15)
St Mary's RC High School, Chesterfield

MY SHARK

I have a little shark
His name is Jimmy Gee
Where did I find him?
In the deep blue sea.
One day when I was swimming
He swam along to me
He asked if he could be my friend,
He was all alone
I said 'I will play with you.'
Until it's time to go home,
Now I see him every day
All we do is swim and play
One day he will grow
And I will have to let him go.

I will be sad then.

Thomas Colin Marper (12)
St Mary's RC High School, Chesterfield

AS I SHIVER IN THE COLD

As I shiver in the cold
I look around and see the world
I think about the winter trees
And everything that is green.
I see two planes crossing,
I hear two birds singing,
I see two trees swaying
And I see two hills above me.

Zara Young (12)
St Mary's RC High School, Chesterfield

WHAT AM I . . .

I swoop and dive,
To wave my stings
I am not a bird,
I have no wings.

I have no ears,
I have no eyes,
I have no head.
So I'm not wise,

Though I sound
Quite sweet to eat,
I have no legs,
I have no feet.

My shape is flat,
Just like a dish,
I'm just a baby

Answer: Jellyfish.

Penny Hodkinson (11)
St Mary's RC High School, Chesterfield

THE HAMSTER CHASE

She wasn't in her cage,
She wasn't in her bed,
She wasn't in the kitchen
So I checked the living room instead.

She wasn't behind the sofa,
She wasn't behind the TV,
She wasn't under the coffee table,
I thought she's hiding from me.

I ran into the dining room,
On my hands and knees
And suddenly I heard a noise
Something like a sneeze.

I began to search quicker
Moving lots of stuff,
There she was just standing there,
She'd been out long enough.

Rachel Brobbin (11)
St Mary's RC High School, Chesterfield

PAIN

Why is pain so hard to describe?
Sharp, talons digging in
Or red hot pokers burning your skin
But the most painful one of all -
Someone leaving you all alone.

Teresa Dillon (14)
St Mary's RC High School, Chesterfield

TRAPPED!

When speeding through the sea,
Searching to kill his appetite,
He comes across a strange sight
And swims towards me.

Behind me is a large cage
And an evil looking man,
I doubt I do not know his plan,
As he stares at me with rage.

I quickly dart out of the way,
The shark swims by my side,
He swims right past as I hide,
In the cage and has no say.

The poor shark now has to adapt,
To its confined surroundings,
The man is pleased with his findings,
So the shark is trapped.

Joy Lennon (12)
St Mary's RC High School, Chesterfield

FRIENDS

Friends are people who are
Always there for you.
Friends are there to make you laugh.
Friends are people who pick
You up when you are down.
Friends are there for a
Shoulder to cry on.
But most of all friends
Should be there.

Cathryn Boyer (15)
St Mary's RC High School, Chesterfield

I DREAMT OF A SHARK

I dreamt that I was on a beach,
With cool sea breeze and sandy feet;
I'd no idea, had not a clue,
What I was just about to meet.

The sun was hot, it burnt my skin,
So I advanced towards the shore;
The cool waves lapped around my chin,
Minutes and I would be no more . . .

I swam around and cooled right down,
The sun then seemed to disappear;
I turned my head - it was no shadow,
A shark was breathing in my ear!

I tried to swim, I only sank,
The shark was gaining on my back;
I screamed, I wailed, I closed my eyes,
Then all that I could see was black.

I'm glad I woke up from that dream,
My forehead - it was boiling hot;
I felt relief, I was alive,
I'm glad that shark was really not!

Bethan Humphrey (12)
St Mary's RC High School, Chesterfield

HEAVEN AND HELL

At the twelfth ring of the bell,
I fell in a hole and went to hell,
When the train reached Devon,
I climbed a ladder and went to heaven.

William Kelly (14)
St Mary's RC High School, Chesterfield

HEY GOD!

I'm panicking, who am I?
Why am I me? Why am I here?
What is in the future for me?
People fob me off with 'Wait and see.'

'My child, you need not worry so much,
No such phrase will I employ;
Your future is always ready to open,
Like a door to either sadness or joy.'

I've still no idea of my future itself.
Unmarried? Wife and three kids?
Who really knows the answer to
These questions? Maybe you?

'You are standing in the doorway
You could walk backwards, you're free.
But if you step in my direction,
You can spend your life with me.'

I can spend my life with you, you say.
In what way? Do I just pray?
Hey, I may need some help here God,
I don't know who you are, or even myself.

'I made you and I love you,
When you're longing, lonely, or upset.
I'm always here - a shoulder to cry on -
And someone to share in the joy that you get.'

A friend for life, and a good one, too.
Yeah, God, I'm liking you more.
I'm newly refreshed, much better than before.
Hey God, you're pretty cool.

Andrew Henderson (16)
St Mary's RC High School, Chesterfield

THIS ONE THING

There are lots of things which interest me,
One of them is supreme,
One of them is majestic.

All is controlled by the click of a finger.

I must be interesting to watch,
Growing, changing, deciding, developing,
Controlled, yet unrestricted,
Free to make the right or wrong choice.

Under this control, this love, this joy,
Warfare goes on, a constant fight;
For what is legally ours,
What is good? Who here is to say?

This one thing, does it sit? Does it stand?
What does it do?
It interests me greatly, the pure selfless love,
Exhibited in the oil painting 'I'

It is not envious, not boastful, not proud,
Not rude, not self seeking, not angered,
It does not remember wrongs or delight in evil.

It is patient, kind, delights in truth,
Protects, trusts, hopes, perseveres.
Is eternal and perfect,
It fascinates me. In the palm of a hand.

Effects, seen like the wind,
It's joy - as tears.
I'm fascinated, mesmerised, perplexed and in awe,
Humble me, show me, teach me, mould me.

All he wants is my love in return?

Gemma Machin (16)
St Mary's RC High School, Chesterfield

THE SHARK

The shark swims along in the ocean blue,
Meandering lazily, nothing to do.
He stretches and yawns and swishes his fin,
There's nothing here to bother him.

A sound he hears, a smell he smells,
No one notices, no one he tells,
He moves with purpose into the shadow's dark,
No sound he makes, no woof or bark.

This fearsome hunter wears the colour grey,
With killer instinct he hunts his prey,
He has razor sharp teeth, and lies beneath the ocean deep
And distance is what you should keep.

In blissful innocence the bright fish swim,
Wrigglingly each colourful fin.
They know nothing of what awaits . . .
Of the terrible doom of all their fates.

The powerful jaw, cutting through flesh,
As wood being cut through by a saw,
The fight was lost before it began,
The shark destroys all, beast and man.

A graceful swimmer,
King of the ocean,
A calculating killer,
But poetry in motion.

Kathleen Lindop (12)
St Mary's RC High School, Chesterfield

ADVENTURE!

At nursery school I'm quiet, quiet as quiet can be,
All the other children run about, every other child but me.
I could go and play skipping with Lisa, Rose and Joe,
Or go play with the water and get soaked from head to toe.
Or dress up as a pirate and go sailing on the sea,
But I don't, I go off on my own, 'cause nobody notices me.

It's so much easier on my own, by myself I pretend it's true,
That I'm a brave soldier fighting a winning battle in Timbuktu.
Sometimes a king with jewels all over, strutting around my palace
And once I was the white rabbit, running late for a date with Alice.
Sometimes a cowboy in the wild west, or maybe a monster in fur,
But most of the time you'll find me, a world famous explorer.

I crawl slowly through the undergrowth, taking care to hide,
Close to the dusty smelling floor, throwing all reality aside.
When suddenly I come face to face with a monster from the deep,
Its golden body lies there, lucky for me it's asleep!
I edge my way around it and slide my feet along the floor.
Oh no! I trip and stumble, and it wakes with a mighty *roar!*

I yell a long loud war cry as I wrestle it to the floor,
But stop at the shadow of my teacher, she's standing by the door.
'How many times have I told you boy? This cloakroom is in a state.
Your mother will hear about this, young lad. Better get
                                        your story straight.'
I turn my back to the jungle, to the magic world I've found
And sheepishly drop Jenny's teddy bear, crashing to the ground.

Clare Livings (13)
St Mary's RC High School, Chesterfield

THE TINY MOUSE

The tiny, baby mouse,
Born into a large house.
The kitchen table,
A large stable,
The garden fountain,
A huge mountain,
A gigantic door
And lots more.
The door mat
A frightened cat,
The breakfast bowl
An enormous hole,
Born into a large house
Was the tiny, baby mouse.

Rocchi Acierno (13)
St Mary's RC High School, Chesterfield

GRANDAD BILL

My grandad's an old man,
When he walks he's as quick as a slug
He's a real skinny person, he looks like a bug,
He's bald with some grey hair round the side
Bill reminds me of a monk or Zinedene Zidane,
He's alright though,
Even though he's got BO!
He gives me money
And he thinks I'm funny,
He used to be a toilet cleaner, that
Gives me rather a chill,
Now you know all about Bill.

Mark Winson (13)
The Meadows Community School

TEACHER BLUES

School started again today,
The kids don't have a bad time,
After all they don't have to teach them,
It's us teachers which have it the worst.

It had snowed in the night,
The first time since we broke up for the holidays,
The kids now don't want to go home,
What's the world coming too?

Got to school late,
The car wouldn't start,
One pupil missing,
They've just had two weeks off,
How much more do they want?

Headteacher impersonator,
Breathing down my neck,
It isn't my fault,
That a pupil is missing.

The third years had a lunch time project,
To build a real igloo,
From the snow on the field,
Trust my luck to have my form in charge.

Now it is hometime,
Time to rejoice,
No more school work
Until I get home!

Adam Smith (14)
The Meadows Community School

MY NEW BIKE

There I was sat in the car
I wasn't going very far
Very nervous in the front seat
I was looking very neat
I was after a giant
Yes, a Chicago giant
One of the best bike brands
In my little hands.
Purple and orange are the colours
Just as good as
My old pink and white bike
Which I will always like
I hope it doesn't rain
Or I'll have to stay in again
Instead of being out
Doing what I like
Which is riding,
Day and night
On my new bike.

Vicki Moore (14)
The Meadows Community School

DOOGLEY, GOOGLEY MOO

Doogley, googley moo,
Googley, doogley doo,
Ping, pang
Twist, twang,
With a bit of woo and boo!

So great is my magic spell,
I think I am doing well,
With my magic words,
I could frighten birds,
Oh! What a wonderful spell!

Frogs and spider legs,
With a mixture of coloured pegs,
With lizard feet
Mmm, I can't wait to eat,
All mixed together with a rotten egg!

Doogley, googley moo,
Googley, doogley doo,
Ping, pang
Twist, twang,
With a bit of woo and boo!

Sinead Roisin Wachlarz (11)
The Meadows Community School

THE ONE I LOVE

I'm in love with him,
But does he love me?
He smiles, waves and says 'hello'
So was it meant to be.
Every time I see him my heart goes a flutter,
Every time I hear him my legs melt like butter,
I think he likes me too,
But I wish I only knew.
He waits for me when school ends
Maybe he only wants to be friends.
If only I knew how to tell him
Things would be so much better.
I could tell him to his face or
Even in a letter,
But if only I knew,
What he thinks of me too,
Then my life would be so much better.

Victoria Limb (13)
The Meadows Community School

MY DREAM

So beautiful I do see,
Through the blurred motion of my eyes,
A landscape of peace,
Full of wishes,
I can rest, be happy and smile again,
Walking through the dreams of others.

Waterfalls, gliding smoothly down,
Clear blue waters,
Shimmering, the brilliance of its glow.
Everything is like this,
Beautiful to the eye,
In my world of dreams.

Where I always am,
Where I always will be.
A land with no poison,
A land that's perfect, in every way,
A land that's just for me.

I know that I'm a dreamer,
But I'll get what I want some day
I'll never leave behind the thoughts that are in my mind.

Kiera Moore (15)
The Meadows Community School

THE STREAM'S JOURNEY

High up in the mountains
Runs a little stream
It looks ever so tame
But when it starts to rain
The crystal clear water turns into a raging torrent
Flowing down the mountainside
Giving wrecked things a ride.

This murky stream,
Is no raging dream,
Now it is a river,
Flowing fast and free,
Out into the far away sea
It quietens, rough no more
Leaving banks an eyesore.

Helen Pearson (13)
The Meadows Community School

PHEASANT OR PRESENT

My dad got me a present today,
A pheasant,
A pheasant!
My dad got me a pheasant today,
As a present,
A present!
It sleeps, it roosts, it pecks, it eats
And when I'm in bed, its tickles my feet.

I've lost my present today, yes,
My pheasant,
My pheasant!
I've lost my pheasant today,
It was a present,
A present!
It used to sleep, roost, peck, eat
And when I was in bed it tickled my feet.

My dad got me a present for dinner
It was not a chicken, or lamb or beef and definitely not pork,
But it reminded me of my other present
It was a big fat, fluffy, plump, cute
Pheasant!

Andrea Victoria Telford (11)
The Meadows Community School

JIM'S BIRTH

At half past 3 on New Year's Day,
Jim hadn't kicked Mum in any way.

All through the night she was getting contractions,
Up to the hospital the petrol was in fractions.

It's half past 5 and they're doing some tests,
My mum's getting scared but she's still my best.

She got transferred to the far away Jessop,
I'm going tomorrow . . . better dress up.

The night after that I couldn't sleep,
I heard the phone go . . . I had a little peep.

I answered the phone, it was my mum,
'Jim has been born, you're welcome to come!'

Nicky Liam Pearson (11)
The Meadows Community School

THE SUN

Slowly at dawn the sun appears,
Lighting up the land where sleep the deer.
Over the river and down the fall
And here the birds do call.

The sun sets over the land
Along the beach and up the sand
Sitting on the top of a hill
Then settling down beside the mill.

At dawn the sun appears in the sky
At dusk it's gone 'oh my'
At which it's time to fall asleep
And count 100 little sheep.

Rebecca Smith (12)
The Meadows Community School

THE HUNTED

You can run,
You can hide,
You know they'll catch you.

You can scream all you want,
You can disguise every move you make,
But they'll know and match you.

They'll hunt you down to the ends of the earth,
For they know who you are
And what you're worth.

They know your face
And where you've been -
Every place.

They'll hunt you,
They'll find you
And they'll catch you.

For this is the hunt,
They are the hunters
And you?
You are the hunted.

Emma Goodwin (16)
The Meadows Community School

HOMELESSNESS?

The cold, the wet, the dreary days,
The ones you don't notice at home,
As I lay awake wondering if I'll survive again,
Waiting, wondering all the 'what if's',
Hoping that the smell of bacon will return.
Wanting, needing, waiting for you to come and take me home,
Back's all crooked as are the cobbled streets,
Sleeping bag's damp, cold and smells like rotten feet!
I hear trains coming in as I lay asleep,
Thinking of who or what I might see,
People give a little change and so I don't survive,
I just thrive on my empty memories as I lay outside.

Rachel Clarke (14)
The Meadows Community School

KISSES

I don't like kissing grandad
He always seems so prickly
I don't like kissing babies much
They are always wet and sickly.
I don't like kissing aunties
Who've got powder on their cheek
I really hate those people
Who kiss you as you speak
I don't like kissing uncles
Who always smell of beer
I don't mind kissing people who've got colds
'Cos they say 'don't come near!'

Nicola Barber (14)
The Meadows Community School

THE MILL

The mill is an awful place to go,
It's better than the workhouse though,
No worker has much light so to us all,
A candle is bright,
The girls are cheaper 'cos they don't like boys,
So we have to work among the noise.
Everyone works night and day,
That's why I ran away,
Over the wall and up the hill,
I'm so glad I got away from the awful mill.

Sarah White (13)
The Meadows Community School

A BEAUTIFUL MOMENT

Red the beautiful red sun set
It feels so warm,
It's shimmering on the
White, soft sand.

The waves are sometimes
Mad but at this moment
They are calm,
They twinkle with the
Sparkle of the sun.

Dolphins jump in and out
Of the waves, laughing,
The wind blows and I
Can hear a sweet song
Whistle all around me.

This is my beautiful moment.

Jasmin Kovacs (13)
The Meadows Community School

QUARRYBANK MILL POEM

I will work day and night,
But I don't have much of a height,
Under the machines I have to reach,
If I get sick they give me a leash.
We have to work day after day,
That's why the kids run away.
It's not a good place to go,
But it's better than the workhouse though.
We live in a small house not ten minutes away,
If we are late, the price we have to pay.

Richard Sowden (13)
The Meadows Community School

DAD'S GONE

I can't believe you left me,
I can't believe it's true,
Mum just said give me the key
And that made me feel blue.
I grasp his ankle,
Please don't go,
Oh dear we're in a tangle,
Then he went, that was low.
At last it was over
My mum was a wreck,
He's gone with a woman to Dover,
I was thinking about him in tech,
The nights are lonely,
I wish he wouldn't be bad,
I wish he'd come back if only
Cos I'm missing my lovely dad.

Keiran Johnson (13)
The Meadows Community School

TONSILLITIS

Tonsillitis, the horrible virus, whoever invented the word,
Whoever it was is out of their mind and utterly absurd!
Tonsillitis, who needs the virus, not me for a start!
Your head is whirling, your throat is hurting and it feels
Like you're being pulled apart.

Tonsillitis, I could strangle the person that ever invented that word,
You're stuck in bed and feel half dead and just can't get
rid of Aunt Merd!
Tonsillitis, what a disgusting word, forever in bed with thoughts
Whirling through my head,
Oh please God please, I'm begging you, can't my sister have it instead.

Tonsillitis, don't say it again, I think I'm going insane,
Nobody wants to know me, they think I'm a big pain,
Tonsillitis, oh when will it go, when will I see the world again,
Maybe tomorrow, maybe in a year!
Will I ever be the same?

Tonsillitis, I've warned you once not to say it no more,
As far as I'm concerned you ghastly, nasty virus you
Can walk right out that door!
Tonsillitis, I'm getting angry now, just go and leave me alone!
Just buzz off and away from here, hurt somebody else's jaw bone.

Tonsillitis, I'm going to scream, how did I get in this mode?
My ears and eyes are hurting like mad
And I'm literally going to explode!
Tonsillitis, I'm feeling short sighted, oh why did I have to lie!
If I have to spend another day in this bed,
I think I'm going to die!

Annamarie Vickers (14)
The Meadows Community School

HOMELESS

The cold wind blows through my hair,
But I can feel it all over my body,
As I walk through the crowd of people,
Its sharp, painful force hits me fast and hard,
Leaving me as cold as a frozen lake,
The rain and sleet makes my feet numb and dead.

No one cares, not a single soul,
They ignore me as they walk past,
Caught up in their own lives,
Too busy to even think about us,
Us homeless, with no one who loves us,
No one who cares where we are.

With no money,
No job,
No shelter,
Leaves you with this empty feeling inside,
You're a failure and you've let yourself down,
You're a loser and nothing will change.

Emma Clarke (13)
The Meadows Community School

A WALK AROUND A RAINFOREST

Tall 'match stick' trees burst through the canopy,
With their leaves, glossy umbrellas of green.
The rigid contours on the butt roots,
Monkeys that wail and scream.

Rope like lianas hang from up high,
Strong enough for Tarzan to swing,
A tropical thunderstorm loiters above
Causing birds to dart and sing.

The dark damp floor of the forest,
The stench of rot lingers around,
Fresh shoots appear, bursting through,
The re-cycled poor soiled ground.

A pig like peccary scavenges for food,
As does the beautiful macaw.
Butterflies, frogs and lizards,
But look closely! There are thousands more!

Mark Ross Pearson (13)
The Meadows Community School

IT'S MY LIFE!

My world seems shattered
And my life seems scattered,
No one seems to mind, no one seems to care,
They think I'm not really in there,
But I don't really care.

I think about people and they don't think
I dare care,
But the love really is there.
My body's battered and bruised
It's aching full of pain,
I feel so all alone
And my heart is frozen like a stone.

I no longer have a friend,
Nobody to rely on.
Everyone says I'm stupid,
Thick or just a prat.
I need someone to help me,
Just love me like my mum.

Laura Beresford (14)
The Meadows Community School

WHY I AM ON MY OWN?

I wish I had some friends but they all hate me.

My teachers call me Einstein and the children
Laugh at me as I sink in my chair.

My class pick on me because of the way I am.

I'm sure my dad does not like me
But I do not say.

I never see my dad, but when I
Do I regret it.

He hits me all the time for no reason.

I wish my mum was here right now.

I try to make friends, but they all
Laugh when I do.

When I am at school, I'm just
On my own because no one likes
Me so I am better off on my own.

That's why I am on my own.

Kelly Collins (13)
The Meadows Community School

HAUNTED HOUSE

I see cobwebs hanging,
On the windows,
I see mice and rats,
Running across the floor.

I feel the cold air,
From the draughty doorway.
I feel the dust,
Being blown onto me.

I smell rotten food,
That is years old,
I smell a musty smell,
From the old decaying furniture.

I hear the mice and rats,
Tapping on the wooden floor.
I hear the creak
From the old wooden door.

Sarah Taylor (13)
The Meadows Community School

IN A CHILDREN'S HOME!

Even though I'm surrounded by people I feel all alone,
Every day I'm wishing that someone could find me
And take me home,
Everybody else seems to be happy and free.
But only me is always wanting my mummy.

The other children seem too young to know,
I am the only one in the home who is always feeling low,
I wish I could forget my mum and dad,
Except I can't they're always on my mind making me feel sad.

I just wish I could forget but I miss them so much,
I wish I could feel their warm soft touch,
If I did see them I wouldn't know what to say,
If they saw me again would they stay or go away.

I wish I could be there in both their arms,
Walking down the street, palm in palm,
What did I do for them to get rid of me,
Mum and dad save me, set me free.

Rachel Adams (14)
The Meadows Community School

BLACK SLAVE TRADE

I feel hungry, thirsty and cold,
But I know I have got to be bold
I know I've got to forget the pain,
Otherwise it will drive me insane.

I can hear people screaming and crying,
I can hear the people dying,
The smell is disgusting and horrendous,
The whites think whipping us is tremendous.

We are travelling across a great sea,
For sale that's what we're going to be,
One day we will get the whites back
We need help from God, that's what we lack.

If they give me just one more whip,
I think I'm going to jump off this ship
They are going to sell us to another place,
All because we are a different race.

We loose everything our family, our home,
Just so another man can have us on loan
Will this pain ever end?
Will we ever find a friend?

Emily Doram (13)
The Meadows Community School

NOTHING

Think of all the people
Who have nothing,
All the people,
No food, nothing.

We take for granted,
The things we have,
When other people,
They have nothing.

We could give the things we have,
Things that we no longer need.
To all the people,
Who have nothing.

Think of all the rich people,
Like you and I.
We could give the things we no longer use,
To all the people who have nothing.

I wish I could help
And I bet you do to,
I could help the people
The people who have nothing.

Daniel Thomson (13)
The Meadows Community School

In The Rainforest

As I lay, I can't sleep,
The noises won't let me sleep,
Birds are screeching in my ear,
Bees are buzzing.

I see a peccary coming towards me,
I jump up a tree,
As I jump,
Termites run up my sleeve.

I feel something sticky on my head,
As I held the tree.
I licked it off my hand,
It tasted sweet,
It was from the leaves.

As I walked through the rainforest,
All I could smell was the dampness
Of the leaves.

As I looked up
It seemed as if the trees
Touched the sky,
As I looked down I could see
The forest animals scurrying by.

Ami Louise Parker (13)
The Meadows Community School

What Could I Do With £1000

What could I do with a £1000?
Maybe buy a mansion or a Porsche,
Or just buy both
Just what could I do?

What could I do with a £1000?
Buy a shop and get lots of chocs,
Naa just get the chocolate goodies.

What could I do with £1000?
Get dynamite and blow up the school
But where do I get it from?
Just what could I do?

What could I do with £1000?
Spend it on PlayStation games,
Or just get a Lion bar,
Now I know what I could do . . .

Leigh Priestley (14)
The Meadows Community School

Bonfire Night

Bonfire night,
Bonfire night,
The stars are bright,
Rockets whooshing everywhere,
The bonfire lightens up the sky,
The words bonfire night,
Came into my eyes.

Paul Hartshorne (13)
The Meadows Community School

ANOTHER DAY AT SCHOOL

Back to school on Mondays,
Get up at eight thirty three,
Dad makes my breakfast
And a cup of tea.
Then I leave, he says goodbye to me,
Walking to school all alone,
Even at school I'm on my own,
All the others I can see,
They just sit and laugh at me,
Through the lessons I listen hard,
Though I find it fairly hard,
I try my best to work,
But they all call me a big jerk,
Sometimes I lurk around
And go places which are out of bounds,
At the end of school I go home,
I get in and I'm all alone,
Until my dad gets in from work,
I just do my homework,
My dad gets in and goes straight upstairs,
I go to bed, my dad doesn't care,
Until it's time to get up again,
Where it starts over again.

Rebecca May (13)
The Meadows Community School

FOR THE FIRST TIME IN SIX YEARS

It's coming up to that time of year again,
No leaves on the trees, a blanket of snow all around
And frost covering every inch of the ground.
The day turning into night around teatime,
Revealing twinkling stars against a black backdrop,
Like icing sugar sprinkled on a cake.
The cold sets in and everyone wraps up warm in
Jumpers, coats, gloves and scarves.
Winter's coming and it's nearly here,
Usually it's the same every year,
But for me it's going to be different for the first time in six years!
As for the first time in six years, there won't be him!
The one I loved and still do!
He was the thing I loved most about winter,
Wrapping ourselves up warm in our jumpers, coats
And each others arms,
Allowing his hand to be my glove, laying in the snow,
Looking up at the stars, with him and listening to him
                              talk about our future,
Before warming up my frozen lips with a gentle, loving kiss.
And I can't ever remember ever feeling more loved and secure.
Now he's gone, I've got no one to cuddle up to, wrap my arms around,
Or hear him whisper 'I love you'
This year I'm going to be lonely,
As for the first time in six years, I'm without him!

Nichola Turner (15)
The Meadows Community School